If My Shoes
Could Talk

IF MY SHOES COULD TALK

Published by Three Eighty One LLC
4690 137th Ave. Hamilton, MI 49419

If My Shoes Could Talk is also available on
amazon.com and e-book thru Kindle

Edited by John Hoogeveen III with assistance from
Jennifer Hoogeveen

Photos Taken By John Hoogeveen III

ISBN-13   978-1482012439 (Soft Cover)
ISBN-10   148201243X
Title ID: 4120654
Religion / Christian Life / Inspirational

Scripture quotations are taken from
-For I know The Plans I Have For You...Eagle Wings Journal.
2000. Barbara Farmer.
-Life Application Study Bible. New Living Translation.
Tyndale. 2007.

Quotes other than my own are taken from
-For I know The Plans I Have For You...Eagle Wings Journal.
2000. Barbara Farmer.

If My Shoes Could Talk

"For we walk by faith, not by sight."
2 Corinthians 5:7

John Hoogeveen III

Others thoughts on
If My Shoes Could Talk

"*The Lord encouraged* me greatly in connecting with John Hoogeveen in WDC as he came 'literally-walking' in obedience to this destination to pray. This book, birthed out of that journey, can instruct all to greater sacrifice from the place of tender love and complete obedience to the Lord God as John models here for us. Approach John's testimony in this book asking the Lord to speak and direct your steps too. May we all respond as John in trusting, expectant obedience."

Lisa Crump
Senior Director of Prayer Mobilization.
National Day of Prayer Task Force

"*John's Story is engaging*, transparent, full of surprises, and ever pointing out God's specific leading and faithful provision."

Pastor John Byker
Senior Pastor Hamilton Christian Reformed Church

"*I was privileged* to see the before and after transition that saw John go from a wide eyed immature Christian into a solid and confident young spokesman to Christians of all ages in just a matter of weeks. John's story is encouraging and honest and was witnessed by many people from Hamilton, MI to Washington, D.C. You will be blessed by his account of this journey."

Pastor Doyle Passmore
Senior Pastor Holland Lakeshore House of Prayer

"*We were blessed* by seeing how God was working in and through John in many unique ways. His growing faith was an inspiration to us!"

Gary Mulder
Washington DC Representative of the Office of Social Justice of the
Christian Reformed Church

This book is dedicated to my Proverbs 31 wife Jennifer and my three children, Blake, Dallas, and Bridger for listening to Gods voice and supporting me on this walk.

IF MY SHOES COULD TALK

A Special thanks to:
My amazing family and friends
National Day of Prayer Task Force
Hamilton Christian Reformed Church
Lakeshore House of Prayer
Gary and Donna Mulder
Pastor Doyle Passmore
Mike and Kathy Wigal
Pastor John Byker
Aaron Brown
Lloyd Kaper
Judy Parrot

Chapters

Chapters

Preface

As I began to pray about how this book should be put together I struggled with what others thought it should be and what I felt God wanted it to be. Should it be a story or should it be put together just like it happened. As I met with publishers and others in that industry most of them thought I should rewrite the book to be more like a story. They wanted me to make it more appealing to readers. I didn't feel that God wanted this book to be necessarily appealing. To be honest our journey with Christ won't always be appealing. My journey was not always pretty. At times it was hard and I didn't even like it. But God always came through and put it all together.

My walk to DC was not about me or even praying for our president. This walk was about Gods faithfulness when we are obedient to His calling. God wanted my experience to get out to others. He wanted people to see what happens when we step out in blind faith trusting that God will provide all of our needs.

So, after a lot of prayer and thinking through I felt that I should write this book just like it happened so you can see how God worked in the moment. Sometimes God worked fast, other times he didn't. Sometimes I knew what God was doing but most of the time I didn't.

So I hope through this journey you are inspired to go and trust God. Even when others don't understand .

We were excited to have Italian sports cars, big houses, no job, tropical vacations and being able to "help" people. We test drove BMWs, Porsches, and Cadillac's. We even walked through multi-million dollar homes. We had pictures of these things and positive sayings all over our house. We were bound and determined to change our life style.

The reality was we never made over $800 in one month. My wife and I had quit after five dedicated years. We lost friends and family because we were so focused on making money. "The business" was all we thought about and talked about.

However, today we believe all that we had learned through this business changed our lives for the better maybe even saved our lives. God knew we were headed down a dark path and sent Nate and Jen to share the business with us for a reason. If it was not for the business I believe I would be in jail, my wife and I would be divorced and our lives would be totally different than they are today.

Today, we have been married twelve years and have three children, Blake, Dallas and Bridger. Without God we would have never made it through all the stress that moving every year, job loss and a large young family brought.

We were married for nine years, lived in eight different houses, had three kids, and I worked more jobs than I can even remember. We always wanted Jennifer to stay home with the kids. We believed that is where a mother belongs, at home with her children.

Life was extremely difficult, but we had each other, and that was all that really mattered.

"What was God doing? Why would he allow us to go through these struggles?" That's what we thought. Now we realize we put ourselves through it! The choices we made had consequences. God didn't put us through it; we did. God got us through it. God was waiting for us to cry out to him. Sometimes it takes hitting rock bottom before we realize that our lives belong to God, once we turn ourselves over to Him we have purpose. We went through job loss, financial issues, moving every year and having a young family so we could share this story with you, a true story of God's grace and love. Christ died for us. That in itself should be enough, but we are sinners and we want our lives to be our own, but they are not. Our lives belong to God.

I invite you to join us in this amazing journey God put us on and continues to put us on every day.

Hold on because it's gonna be a bumpy ride.

Chapter One
Where it all began

The Movies

In 2009 after another last job loss, my ministry started in Hollywood, well, not literally Hollywood, California, but in the movies. I have always loved acting. It's a rush. I started doing background acting in Hollywood movies that were being filmed in Detroit, MI. I was a background actor in big Hollywood films with big Hollywood stars. I was able to share Christ with other actors and actresses. It was amazing how God was blessing me in this way.

Acting was so exciting. Then the film tax credit in Michigan ended and so did most of the filming. No more acting, but that is how God got me excited about ministry; acting ministry is what got me going.

The call to walk
Three years later-2012

Jennifer and I have been praying and listening to God for how he wants to use us. I was working for a great construction company doing historical restorations. I was making good money and enjoyed the work. I was struggling, though, with this idea, this feeling, that God didn't want me working there anymore. I was able to become friends with one of the sub-contractors that worked with us.

We talked a lot about God and Jesus. The more we talked the more I felt like God was calling me to leave. It's hard to explain, but I could just feel a leading from God to leave. Although it made no sense for me to leave, my wife didn't work and we would have no income. I couldn't shake the thought though.

I was led to leave my job in late April 2012. Through a lot of prayer, counseling, and listening to God, it was clear that He was asking me to leave my job.

One Saturday night we went to church, which was not normal for our family. We normally go on Sunday, but the guys and I were going Salmon fishing in the morning. Anyway, in the middle of the service the pastor stopped preaching. He continued to say that he felt led to change the direction of the sermon. He said he had no idea why he felt led to share this story but he felt someone there needed to hear it. He went on to share a story about a man who felt God calling him to leave his job, and this man's wife did not work. That was us! But he had no idea I was dealing with this; no one did, just me, my wife and the guy at work. Unless God was sitting next to me holding my hand and telling me in person it could not get any clearer.

Jennifer and I were doing some local mission work in the small town of Pullman, Michigan. I was feeling led to move from part-time to full-time ministry work in Pullman. After I had quit my construction job things did not start going the way I had planned. I wasn't being used for mission work as much as I thought I would be. I started to question whether I had made the right decision in quitting my job. I knew God asked me to quit my job, it was made very clear. But, if not for Pullman, than what? I started to run, literally. I didn't like running but my wife thought it would be good for me. One day as I was running and listening to a Bible training program, I had the impression to "walk." Not really knowing what that meant, I asked God. I tend to talk to God out loud when I am alone; all I heard was "walk." I didn't literally hear a voice telling me to walk. It was more like an unexpected thought. It was the Holy Spirit talking. "Okay, God, like literally walk or like continue on this spiritual journey kind of like a metaphorical walk?"

I really got no answer. So, I came home and shared the thought with my wife; she really had no clue either. So, I forgot all about the whole walk thing until about a month later when I met with my friend, Lloyd.

Lloyd and I had met in Pullman. We both seemed to have an interest in working with the youth. Because Lloyd had a strong background with young people and has been involved in a youth program for years, we thought maybe Lloyd and I could get together and get something started in Pullman for the teenagers.

We were at Lloyd's house when he said to me, "I feel I need to share with you something I feel God is asking me to do. You may think it is crazy because everyone else does."

I, of course, said, "Okay, what is it?" Lloyd continued to share with me that he felt God calling him to walk, to walk to Washington D.C.

Walk, wait! I heard that word before. About a month ago! It hit me like a ton of bricks. After the shock of both of us hearing the word 'walk' we prayed, a lot.

I came home and told my wife. Although she never said it I think she thought I was a little crazy at first. She told me to keep it to myself for a while!

After much prayer and confirmation through scripture, pastors and writing on the wall, literally writing on a bathroom stall wall, it was clear this was what God was asking me to do, walk to Washington D.C. to pray for President Barack Obama.

Throughout this Journey God used Lloyd to get messages across to me. It was really kind of weird.

The rest of the story is what happened along the way, what God did, and how he used me.

Pre walk meetings
Pastor meeting Aug, 2012

What a great meeting I had with local area pastors. God opened up the opportunity for me to share about the walk that God has asked me to go on with two new pastors and the new director of Love Inc. in Hamilton. Lots of prayers and blessings coming from them. God is so good.

Prayer meeting at Hamilton CRC

What an amazing morning. I went to the prayer meeting at Hamilton Christian Reformed Church this morning and got to share what God is doing in our lives with the walk. Another pastor at the meeting has been praying that our president makes good moral choices. To me, that was a confirmation that I am being asked to pray for our president. God sure puts people in places for a reason. I felt so welcomed there even though I do not attend there (or a Christian Reformed Church for that matter). I felt the way all people are supposed to feel, welcomed, when the body of Christ is at work. What great people at that church. They have committed to being prayer partners with me on this journey. I am excited and blessed!

Pastor John from Hamilton CRC led the Hamilton pastor's meeting I was invited to this afternoon. Wow, me, in a room full of pastors, sharing how God is working in me. I never dreamed this would happen. I cannot wait to see what God has in store for this town, this country, and the Body of Christ.

Training

I had a nice walk tonight of 6.5 miles and felt great. I will be walking no less than this every day until I leave on Sept. 3. I know the blogs have been short, but believe me, a lot is going on. Tomorrow is a busy day. God is working on me and preparing me for what I will come across on the walk.

I really am at a point where I'm like, "Okay, God, how are you going to use me?"

To be honest, the butterflies have started and I am getting to the point where the walk is becoming real for me. "I really am walking 675 miles to Washington D.C.!" I need all the prayers I can get right now. The evil one would love for this walk to fall through, but it won't. Temptations and prosecutions are bound to happen when we decide to follow Jesus with radical obedience. I need to remember that. The devil doesn't like it. After all, we may save some people in the name of Jesus.

I have a second meeting with a family friend and pastor of Lakeshore House of prayer, Pastor Doyle, a meeting with our pastor from our church, Ridge Point Community Church, Pastor Toran, and author and friend Judy Parrott is coming to our home to start the book process tomorrow. Praise God for all the opportunities He has opened.

God still works the same way he always has. After all, God does not change. He stays the same. We are the ones who change. We have to remember who God is and that he is always there for us.

Check this out. Ephesians 4:11-13 *And he gave some, apostles; and some, prophets; and some, evangelists; and some, pastors and teachers; 12 For the perfecting of the saints, for the work of the ministry, for the edifying of the body of Christ: 13 Till we all come in the unity of the faith, and of the knowledge of the Son of God, unto a perfect man, unto the measure of the stature of the fullness of Christ:*

Overwhelmed-Blog Post

My family and I are feeling really overwhelmed with all the meetings I have had and continue to have leading up to the day I leave for the walk. I really never thought that it would be so overwhelming, but it is. Please pray that my family and I have comfort and understanding. For when you live a life for Jesus life may get hard and busy but it is worth it. Please pray that our overwhelming feelings go away and the evil one does not get hold of them. We are going to need more prayer now than ever. Pray for our relationships, ourselves, our thoughts, our actions and our meetings. Please pray that we are guided by what God is asking us to do and keep what is important always in front.

As for me, I need prayer that through all of this I do not neglect my wife and kids. It is so easy to get caught up in "doing." I need constant reminders that the time I do have with my family needs to be spent well and not taken for granted. God has given us more time than normal to be together so I need to use that time. Thank you for your prayers.

Another Amazing Blessing from God

Wow! I have been praying for a small laptop to bring with me so I can update the blog and keep in touch. The Wolters, whom we met at Tri-ponds campground last week, have felt God asking them to help us in some way. They have been praying for God's guidance on how they should help out. A day or two ago they felt God's nudge to donate all the money made from Tabitha's, "Life Expressions" business over the next two days. They have made enough to buy me a laptop and have money left over to bring along. Praise God!

I am so blessed to have met the Wolters, not only for this blessing but for their friendship.

There is no other explanation for all the blessings we have received except that God answers prayers and when we ask we shall receive. Now don't take this out of context. We need a relationship with Jesus and God knows what we need and He knows when we are praying out of a need or just a want and will answer accordingly.

So Blessed

I was blessed Sunday after the church service with a check from a woman in the congregation. With that money I was able to buy good wool socks, pepper spray, a pair of shorts, two shirts, a portable battery charger and still have money left to bring along. Wow, what a blessing. Praise God!

Inspiration

Sometimes God gives you gifts out of the blue. It seems that when we listen to God's promptings and act out of nothing more than obedience, He honors that in more ways than one. Many people have asked me why I am doing this. To tell you the truth, I don't know! Can I see how God could use this? Yes. I could pray for our President and our nation. Can I see where God is using this now? Yes. My relationship and faith in Christ is growing. But, as for knowing the ultimate purpose in detail, I am not sure. I'm not sure we will ever know the full purpose of Gods callings until we get to Heaven.

All I can do is listen, with no agenda, then act out of faith. I don't want what I think should happen get in the way of what God wants to happen. I can go into this thinking, "Oh, I'm gonna do this or that," but God has a funny way of humbling us when we go about our own agenda. God has an agenda for me, for us, and I don't want to get in the way of that.

I was walking last night down M-40 when I came upon three teenagers. I was listening to music but could tell they wanted to talk. So I took my headphones out and said "Hi".

"Are you the guy walking to Washington D.C?" one of them asked.

I said I was; we continued to talk and they asked questions like, "How far is it? How long will it take you?" and so on. It was really cool that God put those kids in my path that day.

One of them had heard me talk at Hamilton Christian Reformed Church the previous Sunday. The gift God gave me that day was that one of them said, "Wow, you are an inspiration. No, really, I am inspired!"

Me? An inspiration? I never, in a million years, would think that I would be an inspiration to anyone. It made me happy. Not that I was an inspiration, but that that these teens were seeing Jesus through me. They may not know it right now but God has a plan for them. There was a reason that we crossed paths. I pray that someday they hear God talk to them and out of faith they act, make a difference in the world and impact the Kingdom of God! We are all God's children and He loves each of us dearly. Just as we should listen to our earthly father we should also listen to our heavenly Father.

Blessed Again

We have been so blessed camping this week. We met some new friends from another church and were able to share about my walk and what God is doing. I am praying that their church will become another prayer partner. God is so good!

Please pray for me as tomorrow I will be talking at Hamilton CRC. Please pray that God gives me the words I need to say and that the glory goes to Him.

Hamilton CRC

I want to thank Pastor John and everyone else at Hamilton CRC for having me share my story. I was able to share with the whole church and answer questions after the service.

It meant a lot to me that I was welcomed at HCRC. I also want to thank Lloyd for being there in support and my small group leaders and friends Mike and Julie Peters.

Extra Blessings

I was blessed today when I got my check for working for my cousin a couple weeks ago. He added extra money for me to take on the walk. Thank you, Ebels Construction; what a huge blessing.

What a Special Morning

I was blessed today by being invited to sit in on the Holland Area Pastors Initiative meeting today. God is doing great things with Holland area pastors. I can sense unity between churches. What an amazing group of men and women. Afterwards I had breakfast with Pastor John and just enjoyed some time talking.

I met with Pastor Jon and Pastor Chris from Trinity Reformed Church in Holland, and they will be praying for this journey as well as putting a write-up in their bulletin next week.

God has used Jon and Tabitha Wolters to bless me with a mini-Dell laptop. We went and picked it up today. It is almost to the tee the exact laptop I had in mind. Praise God!

I want to thank everyone who has helped me so far. All your prayers are felt and noticed. God is really at work here.

Please join me in praying for all those who have been able to bless this journey so far that their blessings on me may turn into blessings for them!

Sunday Morning

Well, it's the last Sunday I will be here until November. It was a great morning. I was able talk about my walk at Hamilton Reformed Church, the church in which I grew up. Pastor Tom called me on Friday and asked if I would be willing to share at the last minute. It was great to be back to see all those I grew up with in church.

Pastor Tom called me this afternoon to ask if I would like him to write me a letter of support from his church. I, of course said, "Yes." How awesome is it that God placed me there, in my former home church, the day before I leave? God's timing is truly perfect.

I feel so overly blessed that there are so many churches involved in supporting this walk. Not only will they be praying for me and my family, but our country and our President as well.

I look forward to saying goodbye to all those coming to see me off tomorrow morning. It will be great to have friends, family, and pastors praying for me before I leave.

Thanks to all of you who have prayed and continue to pray for me as I start this journey. May God bless every one of you.

Chapter Two
EMILIES EGGPLANT LASAGNA

First Journal Entry Since Walking Started
9/3/12   1:55 P.M. Allegan, Michigan
What a great day so far. I am resting at
Emmaus Road Church. My sendoff from Hamilton
Christian Reformed Church was more than
expected. About fifty people showed up including
Pastor Toran, my pastor from Ridge Point
Community Church.

My friend Lloyd, my sister's boyfriend Terry,
my sister Amanda, and my oldest son Blake all
began walking with me. Amanda and Blake walked
the first two miles and Lloyd and Terry for the first
seven miles.

It is really hot, 90 degrees plus. I have already
gone through about 65 oz. of water and a banana.
It's only about 2 P.M.

I'm a little sore but not too bad. I am feeling
pretty good really. I just have to keep praying that I
don't think too much about the pain and I will be
fine.

I have been blessed with more money than
expected. I wanted to leave with $300 and I have a
little over that. Praise God!

9/4/12 7:30 A.M.
Aaron and Emily Brown's home

I stopped by the 50's diner in Allegan last night to grab some cold water and a bite to eat. I didn't want to stop but I just walked up a big hill and it's like 90 degrees out. I felt God telling me to rest.

The waitress asked me where I was going. So, I shared with her what I was doing. I went to pay for my meal and she said it was taken care of! So I left her a $5 tip. As I walked outside I noticed a man in his car with a sign that read, "WILL WORK FOR FOOD." I walked past him at first, but felt I should go back. So I went back and offered to buy him dinner. He said okay, but at the same time another car pulled up. A man got out and handed the man in the car money. I asked him if he was ready to go get dinner, he said yes and got out of the car. At that time, another car pulled up. The driver handed me money thinking I was the one who needed it. I told him that I wasn't but this man did. So he gave him the money. I asked again if he was ready to eat. He looked at me, counted the money and said, "No, I just got enough money to buy food and put gas in my car. You will need your money." What? Wow, God overload.

I arrived and Aaron and Emily's house around 6:30 last night. They had dinner ready for me. Eggplant lasagna, Yum. What a blessing. It was an unexpected jolt to the taste buds!

Who knew a shower would feel so good, knowing it may be my last for a while.

Woke up and ate breakfast, eggs and coffee, good fuel for this morning. I am getting ready to leave and it is raining out. Yuck. Oh, and I have a blister on my toe.

Chapter Three
MOM'S BOSS

3:30 P.M. Otsego, Michigan

I'm in Otsego, Michigan. I just met Dave. He lives here in Otsego but goes to church and preaches in Kalamazoo. Dave seems to be a really cool guy. I shared what I was doing and he prayed with me and even thanked God he met me. God is so good.

Fifteen miles a day is a lot. The last five miles are a killer. I am thinking of doing ten miles a day for the first week until I get used to it, then bumping it up from there.

9/5/12   8:45 A.M.
Comfort Inn, Plainwell, Michigan

I was walking yesterday and I saw this guy walking right towards me. It was weird because he was not moving out of the way. It was my mom's boss! After he had stopped to talk to me, he said he was inspired by what I was doing and wanted to shake my hand, and buy me a hotel room for the night! What a blessing! I got to the hotel and ordered pizza, as this will probably be my last big meal for a while. Of course, that is what I thought about a shower yesterday, too. I took a shower this morning and went to the Laundromat to do a load of laundry.

Pastor John called this morning during the pastor's prayer meeting. I was able to share with the pastors where I was and what God had been doing so far.

9:26 A.M. Plainwell, Michigan

I'm not too far in today, but felt led to stop and enjoy this boardwalk in Plainwell. I'm on a big rock by the river. It is so pretty, one of God's many great creations. It is another really hot day; the cool rock and shade feel great.

11:20 A.M.

I am four miles someplace east of Plainwell on M-89. I am taking little breaks every mile or so; that really seems to help. This heat is a killer.

I just met a really sweet couple. I felt led to go talk to them, so I did. I only wanted a picture of their house. It said "Classic Americana" all over it to me. There was an old 70's car in the driveway, their everyday vehicle, and an old barn with a tool shop. I got the pic.

I grabbed some peanut butter to-go cups from the hotel; just ate one with some jerky. I need an energy boost.

Chapter Four
Exhausted

6:14 P.M.
McDonalds Richland, Michigan

I am really tired! Exhausted! "Please, Lord, remind me why I am doing this. I miss my family a lot! "I am about to cry in McDonald's. "Lord, I just want to sleep! "I am pushing myself to the limit. I have gone 12 miles today so far.

Philippians 3:10-11 says: *"I want to know Christ and experience the mighty power that raised him from the dead. I want to suffer with him, sharing in his death, so that one way or another I will experience the resurrection from the dead!"*

The pain I am feeling hurts. My legs hurt, my feet hurt, and my mind hurts. But my pain is nothing compared to what Christ did for us.

I feel like I am being attacked on the frontline. "I need you, Jesus, NOW! I cannot go through this anymore. I need relief. In the name of Jesus, I ask for relief. I pray for the evil one to leave and for me to be filled with the Holy Spirit. Lord, I need you!" God has done so much already, but this is really hard.

"Please, Lord, give me someone. I need to see you again. I know you are here, but I need to see you!"

I just need to relax. God help me to relax.

8:30 pm

Praise God! I found a place to sleep. A small patch of woods in the middle of town. I am going to pop my tent right here, right now!

9/6/12   3:30 A.M.

Wow, I slept great last night. I fell asleep around 9 P.M. and woke up around 3 A.M. I packed up my stuff and left around 3:15 AM. There was a 24-hour gas station so I got coffee! I am on my way to Battle Creek.

I am sitting at a picnic table at some store; it's about 3:30 A.M. I am drinking my coffee and eating a snack, peanut butter, and some nuts.

Chapter Five
Afraid of the Dark

8:00 A.M. Gull Lake, Michigan

I am about 5 miles in today already. I stopped and took a nap in the woods for about an hour. I found a little spot along the road and popped my tent. Now I am on my way.

As I was walking in the dark this morning, I banged my walking stick on the guard rails to scare off any animals. It at least made me feel safe, kind of like when I was a kid. I would have to feed our barn cats at night. I would run to and from the barn talking out loud or singing to myself the whole time. Okay, so I am a little afraid of the dark.

11:00 A.M.

Taking a rest, I am really tired. One thing I have learned is that ants are no fun. Every time I stop to rest I have ants crawling on me.
My feet hurt really bad.
4:00 P.M. Jim's House

I got my first ride offer today from Jim. I had not planned on taking any rides, but really felt God telling me to take it. I met Jim last night at a restaurant.

I am at Jim's house for coffee. I am pretty sure this coffee is about 5 days old. I took my mace in with me; you never know.

Chapter Six
44 Magnum and Popeye

6:00 P.M.
Econo Lodge, Battle Creek Michigan

Jim had guns everywhere! Three in his garage, three in his car, two in his office. He even pulled out a 44 magnum to show me. Kind of scary, but he seemed okay. He then took me to his barn.... where he had a collection of cars, two Ferraris, two Porsches, three Jaguars, three motorcycles and a trike.

After going back into his house he gave me $100 and insisted on taking me to Battle Creek so I could get a hotel room. What was I supposed to do? I mean the guy had an arsenal in his house. No, he really was a cool guy and I feel God put us in each other's lives for a reason.

9/7/12 8:30 A.M.
Econo Lodge

I slept at the Econo Lodge last night thanks to Jim. I had breakfast at the Pancake House this morning. I learned not to buy coffee from a restaurant, just too much money.

Jim really opened up to me on the way to the Hotel. He said that he has not prayed in a long time and he feels he should start again because his health is not good at all.

10:30 A.M.

I was headed down Beadle Lake Road today, and met this guy in Battle Creek. His name is Popeye. Well, that's what people call him. He is a walker. He has been walking the country for 5 years by choice. He said that he started by jumping trains with a group of train jumpers and fell in love with it. He had dreadlocks, a long goatee about a three- week shave, and tattoos everywhere. His clothing was held, literally, together with safety pins and patches. He was carrying a small backpack and a paper bag. He is headed to Illinois to "The Gathering," a hippie community where there is no money. It works on a barter system and the only "currency" is weed! Crazy! It was 10 A.M. and he was headed to a bush to eat and drink his whisky.

Brady called last night; I was too tired to talk so I will try to call him today. Larry might meet me today that would be nice to see someone I know.

God has placed so many things in my path already, it is awesome.

It is supposed to rain today, looks like I will be getting wet. Oh well.

Chapter Seven
Hillbillies and an Overpass

5:20 P.M. Tekonsha, Michigan

I haven't gotten wet yet. God is so good. I met this nice woman today as I was resting in a church driveway. She gave me $20, cool!

Crazy, I walked past Binder Park Zoo in Battle Creek today. Just realized how far I have made it already, kind of nuts.

Again God is awesome! I walked about 10 miles today and was praying for some motivation. God gave me Sam and Diane. Sam was working in his yard so I said "Hi". He motioned for me to come over by him and we started to talk. He was amazed by what I was doing and said that there was no place good for me to sleep in that area because the hillbillies like to pick on outsiders. He then offered me a ride. He took me almost 15 miles to a roadside park.

I am praying for a roof because it is supposed to rain tonight.

I looked on my phone and realized that two miles up the road there is a McDonald's. I think I will walk up there.

I am at McDonald's resting. I walked under an overpass; I think that is where I will sleep tonight. I will at least stay dry.

7:20 P.M. Truck Stop

I moved from McDonald's to the truck stop across the street so I could charge my phone and computer.

I was going to go to the local high school football game but the high school is too far away, bummer.

It was great; I was able to Skype with Mary and Lenny today.

8:45 P.M.

Well, it started to rain. I still have to walk to the overpass which is about three quarters of a mile from here.

I should be in Homer, MI tomorrow; that's just less than 10 miles from here. Let's see what God has in mind, though. One thing I am learning is that what I think or want may not be the same as what God wants. Things like rides and people giving me food or money always seem to come when I stop trying to find them and give my needs to God.

9:45 P.M. Overpass

I'm under the overpass now. I know I have nothing to fear because the Lord is with me, but every noise I hear puts thoughts in my head.

It stinks under here. I don't know if what I'm smelling is close to me, or if it's a farm.

It's scary under here in the open. When I am in my tent at least I feel protected because I can't see. I will listen to music as I fall asleep tonight.

11:00 P.M.

Okay, should not have had that latte at McDonald's tonight. I am wide awake!

I met this awesome trucker tonight at the truck stop. His name is Sydney and he is a Christian. We talked for a while at the truck stop then I prayed for him and he prayed for me before I left. How cool.

I had about 100 little pieces of paper with Bible verses on them that a friend had given me. I felt led to give them to Sydney. Not sure why.

9/8/12   4:55 A.M.

I woke up at 3:00 A.M. Sleeping under an overpass is about what you would figure. The bed was rock hard and it sounded like a bowling alley every time a truck would go over or under.

I am at the truck stop this morning eating breakfast and hanging out until it gets light out. I figure about another three hours.

11:15 A.M.

I didn't stick to my original route and decided to take a "short cut" today. Really bad idea. I am taking a break right now. I took a nap an hour ago for about an hour. I am feeling really lonely today. No one seems like they want to talk today.

I have been using the woods and corn fields to go to the bathroom. There is nothing out here. I don't want to get disappointed when God doesn't do "big stuff." I have to find the little blessings He gives me. It is cooler today; that is a blessing for sure. I went from shorts and a t-shirt yesterday to long pants and a sweatshirt today. It is amazing how much more I can do when it is cooler.

I am praying for people soon.

What? This was in my journal for today.

Hebrews 13:16 " *Make sure you don't take things for granted and go slack in working for the common good; share what you have with others. God takes particular pleasure in acts of worship…that take place in the kitchen and workplace and on the streets.* "

Then this too! "Many an opportunity is lost because one is out looking for a four-leaf clover."

Wow, that is so me! Time to check myself!

I need to not take my blessings for granted. God gives them to me when I'm not thinking about it. Every blessing is huge and I don't want to expect that God will bless me but to know He can and He has.

2:30 P.M.

I'm really struggling right now wondering if I can make it or not. It's like there are tricks being played in my head! If I quit, what about all those who believe in me and support me? What will they think? Will they think that God isn't faithful? I don't want to dishonor God by quitting.

Why would God have me quit? This is really hard. How do I know what's God voice and what's the evil one?

I can't take this anymore! "God, I need your help! I need an answer! AHHHHH! I sit here wondering what to do. I sit here praying to You. God, show me how; how can I go on? God, give me peace in this place."

Chapter Eight
Soggy Tuna

5:30 P.M. Subway, Litchfield, Michigan
I'm finally in Litchfield, a small little town
with a down-home feel. I chose to take a "short cut"
today. Not a great idea. I ended up walking 5 extra
miles today to get to a town. I took a road that
would "save me 4 miles." That was a long lonely 10
mile stretch with nobody around.

Weather today is great; it is 66 degrees out
right now. This is a welcome relief from the 85-90
degree days I have been having.

Today was tuff. I was close to calling my wife
and telling her to come get me. But Pastor John
called and really helped me get through my struggle
today. God gave me that phone call right when I
needed it. John has become a good friend and a great
support for me and my family. God got me through
my struggle today, I am praying tomorrow is better.

I turn this whole journey over to God. How
awesome. This walk is touching more people than I
expected. The people being touched are why I am
doing this. I am crying tears of joy right now from a
blog comment. This person shared how they have
been inspired and are making changes in their life to
better serve God.

Galatians 6:9-10 *"Let us not grow weary
while doing well, for in due season we shall reap if
we do not lose heart. Therefore, as we have
opportunity, let us do well to all."*

Last Prayer Request for Tonight
8:00 P.M.

Please pray there is place for me to do laundry and take a shower in Hillsdale tomorrow. I stink.

River Front Property

I got river front property tonight. Found a sweet park along a river and found a great spot in the woods. God is so awesome and provides for me daily. Thank you all so much for your prayers.

And Tabitha, your comment was an answered prayer. Thank you! Good night, all. I love all of you.

Emails of Encouragement

E-mail: Hey, Son, make sure you are getting enough sleep and good food. Protein bars are not enough. Glad Lloyd and Pastor John talked with you today. Have a good night and get some rest! God is with you and He will take care of you but you have to do your part! Love and Prayers, Dad!

E-mail: I will be praying for a walking partner for you for tomorrow. Also I will pray that you will be blessed and that you will be a blessing at church tomorrow. I am starting the "Daniel Fast" tomorrow. It is a 21- day fast the way Daniel fasted--only fruits, veggies, and whole grains (no sugar, breads with yeast, meat, or dairy products), only water to drink. During this Daniel Fast, I will specifically be focusing on praying for my family, for church, and FOR YOU! :) If you can walk fifteen miles a day to DC, then surely I can give up my favorite foods! You are an inspiration, John. Hang in there, and I will be thinking of you and praying for you often! Have good sleeps tonight, Tabitha

E-mail: Dear John, I must share this too. Thanks, Tabitha, for sharing your story. I have been struggling lately with really trusting God and letting Him be in control. This morning He told me to run. I haven't ran in a while but it was clear that He was telling me to run. Well, I went out and it was raining and cold. Everything in me said to turn around but then I thought of you, John, and how you are not able to turn around so easily. So I kept going. While I was running, I got sprayed in the face (it was still dark!) by a sprinkler and tripped on a curb. I knew then that God was telling me to keep running, even if it's hard or you stumble. Thank you, John, for the motivation!

There is a huge hill that I always turn around at before I go up it and today during my run, God told me to run that hill tomorrow. May seem insignificant to walking to DC, but it's all about trusting God. Keep walking, John; God is doing more through you than you will ever know! Tiffany

E-mail: Tabitha, you are awesome. I am so glad God had our family meet your family. I can't wait to tell you all the stories when I get back. You too are an inspiration for me to keep going.

E-mail: Tiffany- Thank you so much for this comment. It means more to me than you know. My prayer for you is you not only find the strength to run that hill, but find the strength in Jesus Christ to act for the Kingdom of God too.

Nothing coming from God is insignificant. My walk to DC is no bigger than your run up that hill. When it comes to obedience, God does not favor one more than the other. I think it is awesome that you listened, even when it was hard! You can do it. The hill can't beat you. Through Jesus Christ you can do all things!

9/9/12   8:00 A.M. Subway

I slept in Fireman's Park last night. It was nice. I found a little spot in the woods; there was a river and everything.

I am going to Litchfield Congregational Church this morning. Service time is 10:30 am. This is a random stop so I am a little nervous how I will be received.

Right now I am sitting at Subway eating a sandwich I bought last night. Tuna, kind of soggy.

9:00 A.M.

I am noticing a lot of Amish here in Litchfield. Just saw two horse drawn buggies pull into the store.

10:30 A.M.

This church is sweet; they read announcements. I am used to a large church back home. There are only about 25 people here, so cute.

I met Pastor Mike and his wife this morning. What a nice couple. I feel very welcomed here. God is so good!

The people at this church said that they are happy I am here. I feel so at peace. God is at work for sure.

Things are so "unofficial" here. Pastor Mike read the letter that Pastor Tom from Hamilton Reformed Church gave me in front of the congregation. He then asked me to come up and share my story and what God was doing! So unexpected. But since I love to share my story, I took Pastor Mike up on the offer. It was wonderful to be able to share what God has been doing on this journey with someone besides my journal and the blog.

I have been so touched by the people at this church. I felt the Holy Spirit come down on me today. It was an amazing feeling. I was overwhelmed at times and even had tears in my eyes. I could hardly sing as we were singing old hymns, songs I have not heard in close to fifteen years. But this time, I realized how much God loves me! Overload! Hymn # 565: He Has Never Failed Me Yet. Wow, that touches my soul!
Verses being read in church today:

Isaiah 61:1-3 *"The Spirit of the sovereign Lord is upon me, for the Lord has anointed me to bring news to the poor. He has sent me to comfort the brokenhearted and to proclaim that captives will be released and prisoners will be freed. He has sent me to tell those who mourn that the time of the Lords favor has come, and with it, the day of Gods anger against their enemies. To all who mourned in Israel, he will give a crown of beauty for ashes, a joyous blessing instead of mourning, festive praise instead of despair. In their righteousness, they will be like great oaks that the Lord has planted for his own glory."*

God sent me here today!

Today's service is spot on about church being welcoming to all, being one body, and being Jesus!

I wish I could write down what I am feeling right now but it just wouldn't come out right. All I can say is the power of God is so great! He has shown me His power, mercy and grace today. If I could try to explain what I was feeling, I would say it is like sitting at the bottom of a waterfall letting the water crash onto your face. The Holy Spirit is so powerful that we have no power over Him. He just overtakes our body.

E-mail: Hi John, This is Linda. We met at church this morning. I pray you find a friend to walk with you. You are so awesome. I love your story. I was talking to my brother about you. He believes God called you to "The Walk" because there are probably people you will meet along the way that need to know about Jesus and you will make a big difference in their lives.

I pray you have a safe journey. Keep up the work He has called you to do. God bless you. (The Big Blonde) lol

Chapter Nine
God's Art Work

9/10/12   7:30 A.M.
Lake Hudson. Hudson, Michigan

After taking me to lunch and back to their home to take a shower and do some laundry, Pastor Mike and his wife drove me here to Lake Hudson. There is a State Park here. I walked around for a while trying to find just the right place to sleep. As I was walking I saw deer running; it was pretty neat. I finally came upon a place I thought would be perfect. I was walking up a little hill to the scenic overlook. As I walked I noticed a car with a lady sitting inside. I felt the urge to stop, so we started talking. She looked pretty rough, raggedy clothing, smelled like smoke and messy hair. She was smoking and had pot in her car. She shared a lot with me, not pot, her story. Almost like she had no one in her life. She said this was almost the end. She couldn't take it anymore. That kind of freaked me out. I started sharing with her what Jesus Christ has done in my life and that she means something to Him. She is worth so much to Him. She started to lighten up and began sharing with me that her life has been hard and she had lost a lot. I really just listened. I asked her if I could pray for her and she said, "Yes". After we were done praying she gave me a package of Hostess cupcakes and thanked me. I am not sure why God placed her in my path that day but He did.

I slept on the beach last night by Lake Hudson. Fish were jumping all night. They might as well been sharks it was so loud. It took me forever to fall asleep.

The sunset last night was beautiful with pinks, purples and blues. It looked like a picture out of one of those Country magazines.

Fish are still jumping this morning. They were jumping so much last night you would think they would be tired.

8:00 AM

The scene right now is amazing, a calm flat lake with mist rolling over it. A flock of swans just flew over and landed in the water. The sun rays are hitting the trees in the distance and reflecting on the water; every minute or two a fish jumps and the birds are chirping. If this is anything like heaven, WOW! God is an artist.

Oh yeah, I got poison ivy from Fireman's Park. But, I got lotion for the itch. I guess that happens when you sleep in the woods.

Oh, wow, I just saw a doe and her fawn come up to the water and get a drink. So cool.

James 1:17 *"Every good action and every perfect gift is from God. These good gifts come down from the Creator of the sun, moon and stars, who does not change like their shifting shadows."*

I am about ready to pack up and leave. It is really hard leaving a place because I don't know where or when I will be someplace again. I just need to look forward to what God has in store for me next.

Chapter Ten
Pizza Box

12:40 P.M. Morenci, Michigan

Today is going great! I have to stay in the Word at every break. It has given me strength to keep going.

I am really hungry, only 3 miles until food. I don't really feel like eating my food bars. They get old really fast.

2:00 pm Pizza Box

I am eating at The Pizza Box. It is my last stop before leaving Michigan. I'm here for a couple hours resting. I walked down to the local grocery store to get some medicine. I don't feel all that well.

4:00 P.M.

Lloyd found a church for me to sleep at tonight, but it is too far away for me to get there before dark. I am really tired and do not know where I am going to sleep.

Chapter Eleven
Fighting with the Devil

9/11/12   7:45 A.M.   Just inside Ohio

Last night was awful. I was almost ready to go home. I miss my family a ton, but know I have to go on.

I got sick last night; being sick and not home with your family is no fun. I just wanted my bed and my wife.

There was really no place to sleep last night. I find myself getting forced to sleep closer to homes than I like.

I cried myself to sleep around 8 P.M. after talking with my wife. I wanted to quit so bad. She told me to just go to sleep. I woke up around 5 A.M.

I woke up with an odd refreshed feeling. The only way I can describe the feeling is like God worked on my heart while I was sleeping, because I felt great in the morning. I knew what I was doing and why I was doing it.

9:00 A.M.

I have to wonder, where do people buy food around here? There is nothing around for miles.

I am praying for a family I heard about yesterday. Two years ago 3 boys were kidnapped. Please continue to pray as the family does not know where the boys are.

I am really hoping this poison ivy goes away soon.

I am feeling led to stop by the Mennonite church that Lloyd had contacted for me to stay at last night. I am not really sure why because it is 2 miles out of my way. It should be interesting anyway.

Chapter Twelve
Keys to the Church

11:15 AM Inlet Mennonite Church
Inlet, Ohio

I am at the Mennonite Church. I got here and there was a lunch box with a note on top. The lunch box was for me and there were eight bottles of water inside. Wow, what a blessing. I needed water.

I am going to try to get to Wauseon, Ohio today.

I just met Myrna; she lives next door to the church. She let me into the church to use the restroom. Actually she gave me the keys to the church. She asked if I had planned on staying the night. I hadn't really. She said that if I wanted to I could sleep in the church and she would love for me to come to dinner with her and her family. I wanted to say no because it would be a whole day not walking, but I felt led to say, "Yes".

7:35 P.M. Inlet Mennonite Church

God is great! We just got back from dinner. We went back to the Pizza Box. It was a weekly dinner that Myrna's friends and family have. I felt welcomed. I felt like I was part of the family. God knew I needed a family type relationship.

Being in the church by myself all day was wonderful. I was able to study, pray, and best of all they had a radio so I could listen to worship music. I cranked it up and sang loud, danced and just worshiped God for all He has done so far. It was great.

I am looking forward to tomorrow. What a great little town of Inlet, Ohio.

9/12/12   6:35 A.M.

I slept pretty good last night. The church pews are a little small but at least they had padding. I washed my clothing in the sink downstairs also.

I was able to meet the pastor and his wife real quickly last night. They stopped by the church because I at least wanted to meet them. I mean, they did let a stranger sleep in their church.

11:45 A.M.

I am walking and realized that Wauseon is 10 miles out of my way. Not cool. There are no other towns close by, and there really is no place to sleep on this road. There are a lot of houses and corn fields.

I contacted my cousin Gayle in Toledo. She is going to pick me up today. I will keep walking until I see her. I am going to spend the night at her house.

I am taking a break right now. I wasn't going to stop but there is a row of willow trees, which, are my favorite tree. I had to stop and rest under them.

I am hoping that contacting Gayle was in God's plan. I don't want to take blessings for granted.

"You have a brain in your head. You have feet in your shoes. You can steer yourself in any direction you choose. You're on your own. And you know what you know. You're the guy who'll decide where to go." Dr. Seuss

This was in my journal for today. I believe this is telling me God will bless this whole journey regardless, as long as I listen to Him and my decisions are not bad in nature.

I was a little worried when I found out that Wauseon was not on my way. But God gave me Gayle. I am happy she could come and get me today!

Chapter Thirteen
Thank God for Family

9/13/12 7:00 A.M. Gayle's house
What a great night's sleep. I actually woke up to my alarm. I spent most of my time last night downstairs. I watched a movie and read a little. It was nice to just sit and relax for a bit.

I wanted a ride out of town, but I put this wish in God's hands. It was kind of ghetto where I would be walking. I prayed that if I was to get a ride out of town Gayle would offer one to me. She did. Praise God!

11:00 A.M.
My wife Jennifer got me a place to stay tonight, it's at the Methodist church in town. It's about 12.5 miles from here.

I was walking today and saw a Meijer store. That's the store we shop at back home. I was overjoyed to see a Meijer's. I had to go in! Kind of weird I know. I bought some DVDs because it gets real boring when I am all alone for such a long time at night. 7 P.M. is way too early to be going to sleep. I'm really tired right now, but I have to keep walking. My legs and feet hurt so bad! They are really burning.

Today's verse in my journal:
"If the Lord delights in a man's way, He makes his steps firm; though he stumbles, he will not fall, for the Lord upholds him with His hand."
Psalm 37:23-24
Wow, that is spot on!

Chapter Fourteen
Pistachio Macaroon

7:45 P.M. Grace Methodist Church
Perrysburg, Ohio

I arrived at Grace Methodist Church this afternoon. The people there took me right in. I feel so welcome here. I'm getting used to being gone. I am at peace with that now.

The pastor here, Pastor Dennis, is great! He even went out of his way to get me a TV so I could watch the football game tonight. God is blessing me more than I could imagine.

I went to the local farmers market in Perrysburg, Ohio today. They had tons of free samples! Yum! When you have a very small budget free is a God sent! I had the best cookie on the planet, a Pistachio Macaroon; it tasted like heaven!

I am watching Robin Hood right now waiting for the football game to start.

Through all that has happened I really feel God wants me in D.C. for the Summit. Kim, from the Grace Methodist Church, feels led to give me a ride to Fremont, Ohio tomorrow; that's thirty miles! Eighty more miles and I am half way to D.C. already. God is so good!

Chapter Fifteen
Don't Forget to Have Fun

9/14/12   2:50 P.M. Motel
Bellevue, Ohio

Wow! God is great. I got that ride from Kim today. She is on staff at Grace United Methodist Church. She drove me to Grace Lutheran Church in Fremont, Ohio, where I met Pastor Moren.

Pastor Moren was intrigued by my story and felt led to call Mike. She said that we just had to meet. I'm pretty used to meeting strangers by now. I was excited to see what God had in store. Mike met me at the church. We talked for a while at the church; then he took me out to lunch in Clyde, Ohio. Chinese, YUM!

Mike and I are so much alike it is scary. We have similar family make-ups and we both believe in a lot of the same things concerning our faith and ethical & moral issues.

Mike is in the military and has drill this weekend. Thank you, God, for Mike and all he does for our country.

After lunch Mike drove me here, to Bellevue and bought me a motel room! We got talking over lunch about Christian music and he mentioned that his family was going to see Skillet this weekend. Skillet is one of my favorite bands! He found that out and said, because he had drill he could not go and wanted to know if I wanted his ticket, for free. Sweeeet! Of course I said yes.

Mike is going to talk to his wife about bringing me with them to PointFest tomorrow, which is where Skillet will be playing. PointFest, is a huge Christian concert at Cedar Point. I think God is telling me to have a little fun too.

Mike called; I am being picked up in the morning for PointFest!

9/15/12   8:30 A.M.

I was talking with my wife this morning and remembered this moment. As Kim was picking me up from the church to drive me to Fremont she opened up her back hatch of her van. It was one of those automatic opening ones. Well, I forgot how tall my backpack was and totally ran into it as it was still opening and almost fell over. It was kind of funny.

AHH, another good night's sleep, in a bed! I went to McD's this morning for breakfast. I Just got out of the shower and am waiting to be picked up by Mike's wife to go to Cedar Point. Kind of feels weird.

10:15 A.M.
Still Waiting.

I am a little nervous about going to Cedar Point with Mike's family without him. I want God to be honored. I am praying that he is. I feel this is a God moment but I am still nervous; I think that's okay. I believe I will be tested today, but know through God I will have strength. God put Mike's family in my life for a reason and I want to honor that blessing. Satan wants me to fail, no matter what the cost.

I have God so I am strong. I will overcome whatever is thrown at me because I have Jesus Christ.

"Please, Lord, let me be an influence for You in this family. Let me be Jesus more today than I have ever been. Let others see Jesus through me. Let me love them like Jesus loves. They are strangers to me but yet they are brothers and sisters in Christ. I already feel like we know each other, strange. Lord, help me overcome any temptations today. Bless me and give me wisdom today."

9/16/12   6:20A.M.
Back at the Motel

LAST NIGHT WAS AMAZING! God was so present. It totally felt like I was hanging out with friends and family. We rode rides together and the kids just loved me. We got along great. It was nice to hang around with kids but it made me miss mine a lot. We laughed and joked around like we have known each other for years. They asked a lot of questions; it was cool.

Once we got to the concert the girls left and went to ride more rides. Trish felt comfortable enough with me that she left her son, ten years old, with me at the concert. That was a God thing. Kind of crazy, really, but cool to see how God was working. Her son and I rocked it out to Skillet. It was awesome!

Bob Lenz spoke too. He has a really cool story about his life and faith, he speaks a lot about them at schools. I was able to talk with him for a few minutes after he spoke, to share my story with him; then he prayed for me. Cool, God. Just cool.

Chapter Sixteen
Not so Welcome

3:15 P.M. Norfolk, Ohio

I went to church with Trish and the kids today. Mike was still at drill. I didn't sit with them, though. I sat by another family. After church they ordered pizza for us and we hung out at the church for a bit. I was able to share what God was doing with about ten people. That was really neat.

I got dropped off in Norfolk, Ohio, today by Trish. It was really hard to say goodbye. This family has been like family to me for the past couple days. They showed me the love of Jesus.

I am not sure where I am going to sleep tonight. I kind of feel like staying here but not sure I should. It is already 3:15pm and it will be dark in about four hours. Should I walk or not?

3:45 P.M. Church in Norfolk

Okay. Kind of weird. Sitting inside a church waiting for the evening service to start.

There was a lady there running the hotel (non-Christian) and she said that I should go check with a church nearby. Okay God, I got it. I will stay in town but not sure why, but okay. It's kind of crazy how God answers me sometimes. I am very interested to see what God has in mind. This is church number two with a random stop.

Calvary Baptist Church
Norfolk, Ohio

I was praying if I should stay or not and asked God to give me a sign fast because I was already walking out of town. I felt led to stop at the hotel to check rates. I didn't have a lot of money left, maybe $60.

I am worrying more than I should about a place to sleep tonight. Why? God has come through every other time. What's the worst that can happen? I could sleep on a park bench; who cares, what I am worried about?

The pastor is here now. Gotta go.

5:15 P.M. Hotel in Norfolk

Well, I'm at the hotel. Didn't really have the money but really had no choice.

I knew it would happen at some point. I was not welcomed by the pastor at all! He hardly wanted to talk, let alone let me stay at the church.

Okay, why do I feel like going back to that church? I don't want to go back, God. (As I sat on the bed putting my shoes back on, I was still telling God I did not want to go back.)

I went back! I didn't want to, though. I sat for about twenty minutes in the lobby of a small church without a single hello. Then I met Dwight, an energetic guy who worked with the youth group. I told him why I was there and asked if I could join him with the youth. He said yes; then he prayed for me.

Once in the youth group room he introduced me to the youth pastor. Ends up a girl was there that I had asked earlier in the day, if they had a night service there. She saw me and said that she was glad to see me there. She was maybe fifteen.

The youth pastor even used my story for part of his teaching that night. Awesome! Why do we doubt God?

9/17/12   9:45 A.M.

Yesterday at church really made me realize how much people judge based on appearance. The pastor totally judged me based on my appearance! It was made apparent to me that night that truly following Christ is much harder than I thought.

I think it is sad that when the first thing a pastor thinks is, I don't know this person; he could be a threat; he could be a bad person. Look at what this world has done to us. Even the church is scared.

2:00 P.M.

Beautiful day! It is nice and cool out. Lloyd made a contact with a church today. I am looking forward to meeting their pastor. I am making great time today. At least it feels that way. I started listening to some teachings today; I think those help the time go by faster.

The breeze is so nice to feel right now. I am only about three miles from the church and campground.

It is really hard writing everything down. I wish I could just talk and it would all be written down for me. I just want to catch every moment God gives me.

I am resting under a walnut tree and as I hear walnuts dropping all around me I pray that one doesn't hit me in the head.

Chapter Seventeen
Run in with the Law

6:00 P.M. Indian Trails Campground
Fetchville, Ohio

I was resting at Fetchville Church of Christ when not one, but two police cars pull up! I was waiting for that moment to happen. Three state troopers passed today and every time I was waiting to see the brake lights go on, but they never did. Anyway, the police asked what I was doing and said that they got a call about a guy walking down the road with a big backpack. Apparently that doesn't happen too often here. HAHA. The police ran an ID check and everything. As I was waiting I was able to share my story with them though; that was cool. My ID came back clean, WHEW!

I arrived at Indian Trails Campground. The lady here is real nice. She gave me hot dogs for dinner and even some laundry soap. Oh, the little blessings God gives us.

It is supposed to rain tonight. I am praying I stay dry.

I am really bored right now. The worst part of this journey is when I am alone, outside between 6 P.M. and 9 P.M. There is not much to do for three hours straight. I can't go to sleep too early or I will be up too early.

I am outside at the campground, because I only have my one-man tent so it's not like I can really relax here. I am getting really anxious but can't do anything about it. I think I will walk around the campground for a while.

Looking at the GPS there is really nothing but corn fields all day tomorrow. I'm not liking that too much. Maybe God will get me a ride to Ashland. I guess I will wait and see what God has planned.

I am running low on money. I am down to $28.00. I have to save every dollar for food.

9/18/12   7:00 A.M. Campground

Tell you what; camping is no fun when it's just you. I can sit by the campfire but there is no one to talk to. The campground is totally empty. Missing all of you right now. Love ya!

I'm going to watch some Austin Powers or maybe some Robin Hood.

It's been raining all night. I found out that my waterproof tent isn't all that waterproof. I ended up sleeping in a shower stall of the campground bathroom. I was praying really hard that no one would come into the bathroom that night. I am hoping that the rain stops around 8 or 9 A.M. I am all packed up sitting under the awning by the bathroom.

1:30 P.M.

Well, rain stopped around noon. It was not a fun day! I got pretty wet and I couldn't rest because everything was wet. I walked seven miles straight through in the rain. My feet and legs where killing me, I finally got a break and put my tent up to rest for a bit. I set up behind a patch of bushes along the road, again praying no one would see me.

I'm about ready to head out. I was feeling pretty down because of the rain; I just wanted to rest.

Chapter Eighteen
Feelin' Like A Bum

5:45 P.M. Pump House Ministry
Ashland, Ohio

What a day. I was resting alongside the road and guy stopped to make sure I was okay. He thought I might have been hit by a car. I was lying down. When he found out I was okay and headed in the direction of Ashland, he said that was where he was headed and he offered me a ride. He drove me to the Ashland County Fair. I walked around for a little while but they had more food there than anything else. I ended up having a fish sandwich.

Lloyd got in touch with Pump House Ministries today. I guess it is a homeless shelter. So that is where I am, waiting for the guy in charge. When I talked to him he seemed like he had no idea what I was talking about. He sounded really stressed and really busy. I think I am staying here tonight but not really sure.

My feet hurt extra bad today; I walked a little over fifteen miles. I'm in pain!

The weather tomorrow is supposed to be nice. It is getting cold right now and I have had no word from this guy. I think I will try to find a place to get warm clothing tomorrow.

First time I'm feeling "homeless." The guy I am supposed to meet is still not here. I have been waiting for over an hour.

Found out the lobby doors where unlocked. I am now sitting on the floor, still waiting for this guy. It's been about an hour and a half now. At least it is warm in here. I am not really in the building, though. It is more like an entrance before the real entrance to the building. This is the first time I feel unsafe. I am in a big town with very little protection and it is now dark out. Kind of feel like a bum.

E-mail: I hope the rain stopped and that you got to see the same beautiful rainbow that we saw in Michigan this morning! Someone said it reminds us of God's promises. I agreed that it made me think of that, too. It also made me think of my science lesson today and I ran down to the office to grab a camera so that I could explain the science behind rainbows, too! Ellen

9/19/12   7:00 A.M.
Well, I slept on the concrete floor last night. The guy never showed up and I fell asleep waiting for him. I woke up this morning to a guy asking me if I was the guy walking to Washington D.C. He said that they were expecting me last night. I told him that I had been there all night.

He brought me inside and got me some coffee. Inside I met JR. God sent me JR. He offered me more coffee and some cereal for breakfast. We started talking and I found out that JR is a drug addict and alcoholic. He is going through detox right now. He hasn't slept in three days, at all.

It is weird being in a homeless shelter. Everyone here is so encouraging to each other. They are all here for the same reason, help. They need Jesus.

I prayed with JR that his detox is as pain- free as possible and that God helps him. He said that he struggles with religion and God and he only prays when he is in trouble. I was able to share the grace of God with him. God is so good, I am happy this door was opened.

Being here made me realize how much we take for granted. JR is happy with working for room and board and $100 in food stamps! He is truly grateful. How many of us would complain?

This is not a church but I still feel the love of Jesus.

Wow! I am sitting here with a group of addicts and homeless guys. What a comforting feeling, odd.

It is amazing; when you are alone, race, money, looks, none of this matters. All you want is relationship. Why don't I do this daily? Jesus did and I must too!

I think we get so caught up in our lives we forget about the world, at least the part that doesn't "benefit" us. Jesus spent time with the least of us; that's what we need to do too.

I just talked with Trish. I am looking forward to hearing from Mike; she said he is going to call me today.

My daughter Dallas was worried that I would go without coffee. I have had coffee every morning since I left. No need to worry.
Thirteen people live at the Pump House Ministry Home. They are all really proud of the water filtration systems that they make and send to Kenya.

JR asked me to stay for lunch so I am going to do that, then be on my way. The church in Rowsberg fell through so I am not sure where I am going to sleep tonight again. Oh well, maybe I can stop by some Amish place and sleep there.

I was about ready to leave when JR came and sat by my table where I was reading. We talked for a little while. I was able to share more of God's story with him.

I am feeling led to ask JR to come with me. WHY? "Please, God, help me here. He has an addiction problem and he is on meds; this doesn't seem like a great idea. I can't get this out of my head."

3:00 P.M.

Well, I left the homeless shelter but God told me to turn around and ask JR to come with me. So I did. I didn't want to, but I did. And JR said he couldn't. I knew he would say that. But he looked at me with tears in his eyes and said, "I love you, man; you have to come back here, you just have to."
What, God, what was that? So I hope someday I can make it back to Pump House Ministries to see JR.

Chapter Nineteen
Ole' Zen Hermit

4:55 P.M.
Prayer is amazing! I'm in Wooster, Ohio. This is my half- way point! I have been gone for only two weeks and two days. Thank you, God, for all the blessings. Looking forward to my first shower since Sunday morning.

Email: WOOT! That is great! Praying for the second half of your journey!
Tabitha
Email: Good to hear you are at your half-way point!!! May you be surrounded by loving people along the way. :) Karen

6:09 P.M.
Email: Thank you for all the updates! I continue to lift you up in my prayers...may God BLESS you and keep you healthy, may He keep your spirits up and give you strength for the journey!! Blessings!! Deb

7:55 P.M. First Presbyterian Church
Wooster, Ohio
I'm at First Presbyterian Church in Wooster, Ohio. Lloyd made this connection for me.

I was walking and praying that God would get me a ride today. I didn't leave Pump house Ministry until after 3:00pm, so it was late in the day. As I was walking a man stopped and asked where I was headed and if I needed a ride. He said that he was headed in the same direction I was going. I didn't really want to take the ride but I did pray for a ride, so I took it. This is the one and only time I accepted a ride from a total stranger that stopped along the road.

It wasn't until I got in the truck and we were headed down the road that I realized he had been drinking. His breath smelled like beer and he offered me one. He was a very outspoken person. When he found out what I was doing he went on a drunken rant (but positive) about how he was used by the Lord to pick me up and God used him to bless me today and on and on. He was pretty funny. I was a little scared for my life, but he was funny. He drove me to Wooster.

When we got to my drop-off point, he slammed his brakes on and almost shoved me out the door, but not before he fist-bumped me and kissed my hand. I was creeped out! He smelled like alcohol! We were in a beat-up Ford ranger. And he had to tell me he had a gun and was not afraid to use it. Yikes!

When I got out of the truck he shook my hand and said something in a slurred drunk voice. I'm not real sure what he said. I did make sure to remind him that my bag was in the back and not to drive off with it.

When I arrived at the church I met Bob. He is a janitor here. He is a talker; will just about talk about anything. Real nice guy.

9/20/12 11:00 A.M.

I spent the morning with Bob. I had to mail some stuff home so he walked me down to the post office, then we walked downtown Wooster for a while. It is a beautiful town. Now picture this, a thirty-year-old wearing wind pants, an old ball cap and a sweatshirt walking with a sixty-year-old hippie with a long white beard, long white hair, old torn dirty clothes and a very old, worn and dirty ball cap and a walking stick. That was us this morning.

Bob introduced me to Kathy, a lady who works in the daycare here at church. We connected right away; I was able to share my story with her and three other girls in the office. Kathy called her pastor and he prayed for me over the phone. Kathy then called the youth pastor at her church; we have a meeting tomorrow.

Kathy offered an empty apartment to me for the night. That is where I will be sleeping tonight. I might be in town all weekend. They want me to walk in a Heart Walk with them. That is on Saturday. I am leaving it in God's hands, though.

When I was over at Bob's house he read the Bible to me, in Greek. That was cool. He is a very educated guy, it seems. Bob claims to follow the way of the Buddhists and doesn't really believe in God or want anything to do with God at all.

I am so tired right now, overwhelmed by what God is doing!

3:30 P.M.
A lot of churches around here have big wooden doors, so uninviting.

5:15 P.M.
Bob calls himself the Ole' Zen Hermit and he calls me the Zen Christian.

I got a phone call from my wife today. We were blessed with $150 yesterday and $365 today from people who felt led to give to us. WOW! I was down to $5 and was totally relying on God to provide, and provide He did! This should last for a couple weeks.

9:20 P.M. Mike and Kathy's House
I'm at Mike and Kathy's house. They had dinner ready for me and everything, grilled chicken, mashed potatoes and corn. It was my first home-cooked meal. I spent a couple hours sharing stories from my journey with them and they shared stories about their Amish friends and Mike's heart transplant. They have started a ministry for people with transplants, so cool. Mike speaks at schools about organ donation and how important it is. There is a heart walk this Saturday that Mike started; there will be around 200 people there. I have also made the decision to walk in it with them.

Mike and Kathy said I could stay as long as I needed to. Bob thinks that Mike will drive me to Washington; we will just have to see what God does. Tomorrow I meet with Jeff, Mike and Kathy's youth pastor. I am excited to see what happens. I have a whole apartment to myself, cool.

Email: All I can really say is, "Amazing." If you have hard days ahead, remember these amazing moments that God has given you, and that will help you through the tough times. Will be praying for continued amazement from God!   Tabitha

9/21/12   8:30 A.M.
I slept great last night. Today is the first time the sun light woke me up and not an alarm or the hardness of the ground.

The water here smells like sulfur. I'm not complaining; having a shower and toilet is awesome, I'm just noting.

Kathy and Mike want me to stay for a while. I would need a good reason to do that. Mike would have to give me a pretty good ride to make it in time for the Summit. Praying hard about this one.

I talked with my wife Jennifer about walking in the heart walk this Saturday. She is very excited about it and thinks it would be cool. Whenever she is excited about something that always means a lot to me.

11:00 A.M.

I met with Jeff this morning. He is a real cool guy but not much came out of the meeting yet. Not sure what God is doing with that meeting. Jeff dropped me off at the Wooster Library. I walked around town a little and stopped into a couple antique shops to look around.

I am back at the library waiting for Mike to pick me up. I am still not sure about this weekend or what God has planned. I don't want to stay here all weekend for nothing. I'm sure tomorrow will be fun with the walk and all.

I probably won't leave until Sunday or Monday. I really need God this weekend to amp things up.

There is only twelve days until the start of the Summit. What do you want, God?

Faith, what is faith? It is not only believing in Jesus, but acting like Him and trusting that God will come through even when we can't see. Without the action of faith, faith is dead.

James 2:26 *"Just as the body is dead without breath, so also faith is dead without good works."*

1:00 P.M. Bobs House

Bob asked Kathy for me to come over again today.

Hanging out with Bob again today. He is showing me videos of himself on the beach in California and talking about movies.

He is looking at my blog and asking a lot of questions. It has been really cool day so far. I am sitting in Bob's living room on a rocking chair. Well, it used to be a rocking chair; it has no legs. Bob also calls me the pilgrim. He is telling me about Mike and Kathy right now. Such a great guy. We are looking on Google maps right now. He has never seen this before and is amazed by it. He is showing me the house where he grew up in in New York.

Bob found out that I did not have enough money to get into the Summit. He told me I should pray to God for the money. What. Crazy that Bob told me to do that. So, I asked him to pray with me. To my surprise he said okay!

9/22/12

Email: Hi John, Just wanted to say you are loved and I can see through your blogs that all things work out for the best by trusting in God to fill your needs. Looking forward to more, loving the pics too. Have a great day! Linda in Litchfield

Today is going to be great. We have the heart walk for the American Heart Association today. After we are done "working out" we are going to Bob Evans for breakfast.

After the Heart Walk I spent time with Matt and Dana (Mika and Kathy's son and daughter in-law). I met their kids and went to their house. Mike took me into the woods to check his trail cam for hunting. I felt so welcomed by him, almost like a brother. We went to MC Sports and Wal-Mart so I could get some warm gear. I bought gloves a hat and long johns.

Today there is a mission thing at the airport called Missions at the Airport. There are about twenty different missions there and a chicken dinner. I am going with a couple I met through Mike and Kathy, Tony and Mary Ann to see if I can make any connections.

9:00 P.M. Mike and Kathy's House

What a great day! After all the stuff during the day I got to spend time with Mike and Kathy's family and friends at a party at their house. We had chili, taco salad and an amazing buffalo chicken dip that Mike and Kathy's daughter-in-law Jenn made. Thanks, Jenn.

It was great. I was laughing and hanging out with "family."

I am praying right now that God shows me how long He wants me here. I feel He is not done with me here yet but not sure what for yet.

Matt and Dana are on fire for the Lord. I am excited to go to their church in the morning. I pray that God answers some prayers there.

I have been in the Wooster area since Thursday, almost four days. By the time I leave I will have been here five days. Why so long? Am I here for me or for someone else? What is it?

I struggle with wanting to leave so I can continue on but want to do God's will.

"Oh, Savior, what do I do? I am torn between two. I want to go but also want to stay; oh, Lord, what do I do?

I lay here wondering if this is You or me. My mind races back and forth. Lord, please rescue me from this confusion. Show me, Lord. Show me, Lord. All I want to do is to obey you."

I went to the Missions at the Airport today. I think I went so God could show me that I am not being led into "Corporate Missions". At least not right now.

Email: You got it, Son; we are all praying with you and for you! Also praying for your new friends! Love ya! Dad and Mom

9/23/12 4:00 P.M.

Email: Good morning, John. I woke up this morning with you on my mind. I've been praying for you and I feel I need to send a prayer your way so here it comes.

Dear Heavenly Father, I want to thank you for the opportunity you have given John; thank you for all the people he has met and all the blessings he has received. I ask, Lord, that you continue to keep him safe as he travels on this journey. Lord, only You know what's ahead of him. Help him to clearly hear You so he may be obedient to you. Also, Lord, be with John's family, as they are on this journey also, not physically but mentality and spiritually; bless them Lord, as this journey continues. Amen

John, have a great day. I'll be praying for you and keep the blogs coming.

P.S. I'll also be praying for your friends J.R. and Bob.

Great day at church today. The Holy Spirit really touched me today. I learned about Daniel and how he never wavered from God's calling I want to be like him.

I went to lunch with Matt and Dana after church today. We went to a great Mexican place. They treated me. I had chimichungas.

I spent a lot of time with Mike and Kathy's family today. What an amazing family of God.

Mike just told me he feels led to drive me to Washington, PA. tomorrow. Now I don't know if it was God or the fact that there is Cabelas in Wheeling, WV. HAHA. And no I did not tell them that Bob felt Mike would drive me to Washington. Pretty neat how God works huh?

I am pretty exhausted tonight; shared my story with a lot of people today.

10:00 P.M.

I am just now going to bed. Mike and Kathy really opened up today about Mike's heart transplant. They showed me a movie Kathy made about it.

Mike and I really get along well; we are to the "picking on each other" stage now. It really feels like family here.

This family's really means a lot to me, and I hope I see them again.

I am excited to spend the day with Mike tomorrow. We will be stopping by Cabelas in WV.

Chapter Twenty
Amish Country

9/24/12 10:30 A.M.
Well, on my way to Washington, PA. with Mike. We stopped by Kathy's work to meet the church staff. Bob was there. He gave me $150 to get into the Summit. Nuts.

We are in Holmes County, Ohio, Amish country. We have stopped at Mrs. Yoder's for lunch.

Wow, I just ate the best meal ever! Everything here makes me want to slow life down a little.

We are going to stop by Heine's Cheese Factory today to sample some cheese.

Wow, the cheese here was awesome! My favorite was the Cappuccino Cheese and Smoked Cheddar and Swiss.

I wish I could explain the views here in eastern Ohio. I have one word, breathtaking.

Chapter Twenty One
Washington, Pennsylvania

5:30 P.M. Motel 6

I arrived at Motel Six in Washington, PA. It looks like there are a lot of construction workers here.

I just talked to one of the workers; I think I could have gotten a job working on the pipeline. He said they are behind and asked if I was hired on or not. He also offered me a ride but he is going in the wrong direction. Oh, well. Not God's plan.

I ordered pizza for dinner tonight. It gets real lonely sitting in a motel room eating pizza by yourself. I am so thankful I have a family back home.

9/25/2012 9:30 A.M.

Well, I'm on my way headed down Highway 40. I stopped for breakfast at a small joint. Prices seem high in PA.

I am feeling a little anxious about the mountains but I know God will protect me. I am really missing Jennifer right now.

I just got a text from Kathy; she said that a lady she knows in Wooster asked if I was an angel. Funny, never been called an angel before.

Trish McElfresh has become quite a good friend. She is the one who I went to Cedar Point with. It is nice to have people other than family to stay in touch with.

The message God has given me so far is of faith and trust. God will always be faithful.

I am feeling the need to fast. Water only for two days. "Lord, confirm this in me. I need to draw closer to You. I will need your strength and power to go through the mountains fasting for two days. Lord, I commit this fast to you. If Jesus fasted then so can I. For I can do all things through Christ who gives me strength. Show me, Lord, today and tomorrow what I need to learn; guide my feet and my mind. Give me wisdom, Lord, to see. Amen."

9/25/12   12:30 P.M.

I am feeling great; I started listening to worship music and singing. Clouds have rolled in but no rain yet.

Chapter Twenty Two
Mini Church in Pennsylvania

12:45 P.M.

I have been praying all morning for a place to rest. I just came upon a nice little Methodist church! They even have outside plugs so I can charge my phone and computer. God is so good!

They have a cute little prayer chapel here; it is like four feet tall but open 24 hours. I could sleep here but it is only 1 P.M. What do I do?

There is a Bible open to 2 Corinthians 6 in the prayer chapel and it reads: *"As God's partners, we beg you not to accept this marvelous gift of Gods kindness and then ignore it. At just the right time I heard you on the day of salvation I helped you."*

WOW! I am staying here for sure. Thank you, God.

This is nuts; how many churches have a 24-hour prayer chapel? God totally answered my prayer, super cool.

I get God-time, rest, and I stay dry. I should be in Maryland no later than Sunday, as long as I don't get side tracked. God has a way of getting me where I need to be when I need to be there.

Forecast says rain all night, starting at 6:00 P.M. so He gave me shelter just in time, again!

It is hard fasting. The evil one tries to get me to fail but God is stronger. Yes, I am hungry but that's okay. It makes me turn to God.

I am fasting for peace of mind as I walk through the woods and so I can focus on God, talk to God and listen to God.

Lindsey Storm just sent me a message that she will be in New York around the time I plan on leaving D.C. I am praying that God answers why I need to know this.

I am hungry; fasting is harder than I thought it would be. I'm not sure how Jesus did this for forty days!

I am tired, but I know that if I fall asleep now I will be up 'way too early.

I really have to pee. I am waiting until dark so I can go behind the building.

Played solitaire on my computer for a little bit tonight, but that got boring fast.

I talked with Lloyd again today; he is going to try to find me a place to crash for tomorrow night.

Pennsylvania is pretty. More hills to climb, but pretty. I'm about fifty miles outside of Maryland. That's less than 200 miles to DC.

I'm sleeping in the prayer chapel tonight. Not a real active day but the weather was great so I was blessed.

Sleep tight, y'all.

9/26/12   2:00 P.M.

I have been walking all day. It rained until noon and is still misting. I still have no place to sleep tonight and I am eleven miles in for the day. I am feeling great, though. I am eating lunch at a little restaurant called Hugo's.

I should be in Uniontown, PA. tomorrow night. I have a big mountain to climb soon, though.

As I was walking today a guy gave me some apples from a fruit stand he runs. There are great people in the world.

God has given me a lot of energy today. I am trying to figure out why.

I was not able to fast for two days, but I did fast for one full day. It probably wasn't a good idea on my part to try to fast for two days before I had to climb a mountain.

3:30 P.M.

I'm on my way from lunch now. Lunch was great.

For some reason my left pointer finger hurts really bad. I'm not sure why.

Praying for a place to sleep tonight.

Wow! God is great. I just had my lunch paid for by a total stranger.

Chapter Twenty Three
Tornado Ally

7:00 P.M. Union Town, Pennsylvania

As I was walking through Brownsville, Pa yesterday I had to cross a bridge that had a NO PEDESTRIAN CROSSING sign on it. Once I got to the other side, the fire department was waiting outside for me! I guess a kid saw me walking the bridge and told the fire department. Apparently there are a lot of people who jump of that bridge and they were afraid I was going to jump.

God answered my prayers for shelter tonight. I met some amazing people at McDonald's. They said that if I go to their Bible study they would find a place for me to sleep. So I'm at their prayer meeting and just found out that this lady's husband works in D.C.. Crazy. God answers prayer! I'm not sure why this is such a surprise every time. I know He does.

I just realized I have walked eighteen miles today! This is the most I have walked in one day. Weird, I wonder why God has given me so much energy today.

9/27/12 7:30 A.M.

I stayed at Sharron's house last night. I guess they have some homeless guy living with them, weird. He smokes, a lot, in the house. Yuck! He was coughing his lungs out last night. I had to put a pillow in front of the door so the smoke didn't get into the room I was sleeping in. I think my headache I have this morning is from that.

Holy cow! I just heard on the news that there was a tornado in the town I would have slept in last night if I hadn't walked eighteen miles! God saved me from a tornado!

I am going to have Sharron drop me off in Uniontown. I may stay there tonight; it is supposed to rain all day.

Email: Amazing! How cool that you were able to stay with someone you MET at McD's!! Sweet! Continuing to pray for you! Had Jennifer over today, and it was wonderful to chat with her and hear how the family was doing, and hear a bit more about your trip. We can't wait to have your whole family over to our place when you get back and rested. Continuing to pray for you...praying specifically that God will give you much endurance tomorrow! Blessings! Tabitha Wolters

Chapter Twenty Four
Blue Mountain

9/28/12   9:30 A.M.

I stayed in a cute little motel last night, the Blue Mountain Motel. I stayed there all day, as it rained all day and I was really sore and tired.

I could see the beautiful mountains from my room. What an amazing sight. I am still very tired and sore but I have to go.

Praying that Sharron's husband picks me up Sunday, but that is all in God's timing.
My legs are really sore and my hand still hurts. I wonder if my hand hurts from using my walking stick.

I am waiting to leave my motel room until the local restaurant opens at 11:00 A.M. It is a buffet. I'm gonna chow. I am not planning on any food until tonight.

I am looking out of the window and there is mist coming off the mountains, very peaceful.

As I have been led to churches and people I have been led to more youth pastors. I wonder if God is trying to tell me something. Pastor John called today and he wanted me to talk to the youth at his church once I get back.

9/28/12 12:45 P.M. Mt. Washington

I made it! My first real mountain. I climbed Mt. Washington - elevation 2450 feet. God is so good. There is so much beauty in this world.

I am on my way to Saint Joan of Arc Church. I will be camping out in their yard tonight.

I just met this awesome kid, Taka, at subway. We had lunch together. I was able to share my story with him and he shared his with me. He just came from New York and is on his way home to Oregon. He is feeling led to be a youth leader back home. Please pray for a safe trip home for him and that God guides him in the right direction.

I am so blessed to be meeting so many good people. God is amazing!

Chapter Twenty Five
Deer John

5:30 P.M. Fort Necessity, Pennsylvania

I was walking through Fort Necessity this afternoon when I walked up on a buck and two doe. I was like thirty yards away before they even moved. I thought they were fake.

One thing that I love is when people honk. I don't know if they honk and wave because they know what I am doing or not but it still makes me happy.

I'm sleeping in my tent on the grounds of a Catholic Church tonight. I feel safe here.

I mentioned that I had met a cool kid named Taka at Subway. He sat down and had lunch with me. Before he sat down he ran out to his car. Once he returned he gave me a big bag of chocolate covered almonds and $8.00. He said he has been gone for months staying with friends in different states. He said that I have inspired him to pray more. That's pretty cool. Of course it has nothing to do with me, but with what God has allowed me to do.

I went over to the BBQ area at the church tonight to plug in my computer so I could watch a movie and study a little. It was kind of weird watching a movie outside at a church I have never been to before.

Chapter Twenty Six
Uphill from here

9/29/12   9:30 A.M.
It got cold last night, upper 30s. Brrrr. I packed up and headed out around 7:30 A.M. I'm resting alongside the road right now overlooking a golf course. The fall colors are beautiful and the clouds are going through the mountains. The beauty God created takes my breath away. I wish I could package this up and take it home with me.

11:00 A.M. Not real sure where I am.
Well, it's pretty much uphill all day from here. I stopped by Carl's Family Restaurant for brunch and met a lady who saw me walking up the mountain yesterday; she lives in D.C. She said that she is going there tomorrow and maybe if she sees me she will pick me up.

It has been a pretty rough morning on my legs, glad to be taking a break.

5:00 P.M. Addison, Pennsylvania
Today was a tough climb up the mountains. My legs are killing me. I made it to Addison today, about thirteen miles. I'm at the Addison United Methodist Church. I'm camping out back. No one knows I'm here. It seems kind of weird but I feel God gave me this place today. I am just hanging out in my tent waiting until dark. I don't really want to be seen so I can't do much so I'm hanging low. I just hope it doesn't rain tonight.

As I sit here I'm waiting for the cops to show up or something. I feel real uneasy all of a sudden about this but there is no place else to sleep. The roads around here are built up so I can't just find a spot in the woods, I'm in the mountains.

I was so tired today walking up the mountain that I rested in a ditch.

Email: I do hope you find a church to go to tomorrow. However, if you don't, remember that you are in God's church right now! What an awesome way to worship his blessings-outdoors, in the beauty of the mountains. Ellen
6:00 P.M.

I found out today that Highway 40 is the first national highway in America. George Washington, before he was president, made this road with his army. I think that is pretty neat.

Chapter Twenty Seven
Gods Perfect Timing

9/29/12   6:30 P.M. Grantsville, Maryland
Unreal! I was resting at the church and was going to sleep there. Then, I suddenly felt a strong sense to leave and leave now. So, I packed up my stuff and left. I wasn't really sure why but I did. I was praying to God why he would have me leave; after all, I had a place to sleep. As I was walking I was hungry and praying for food. Just ahead I saw a bar. I thought there had to be food there. I walked up to the door and had a strong sense not to go in, so I didn't. I started walking and felt God tell me to turn around and go back. As I walked into the parking lot a black car pulled in with a couple in it. They asked if I was John. It was the pastor and his wife from the church I was just at. It was a church that Lloyd had contacted but only left a message with. I did not know this. The pastor said they saw me walking and when they got home and heard the message from Lloyd they knew that it was me. They bought me dinner, a motel room and gave me $20 for food. God is so good and his timing is always perfect. None of that would have ever happened if I had not have left the church when God told me to. I could have totally missed this God opportunity!

9/30/12 8:30 A.M. Penn Alps

I slept at Casselman Inn last night in Grantsville. It was another cute little motel. There seems to be a lot of those around here and cheap too. I was at Penn Alps eating breakfast this morning, all you can eat buffet for $6.95. I met this nice older couple there. We were talking and they told me that they saw a black bear up the road this morning. I kind of hope I see one, not too close though.

Amazing, I felt led to pay for this couple's breakfast this morning, so I told the waitress that I would cover it. The couple and I started talking and I was able to share more of my story with them. Then without them knowing that I paid for their breakfast they gave me $20.00!

As I was leaving I met another pastor in the gift shop. We got talking and I was able to share with them what I was doing. She prayed for me and then continued to pay for both my bill and the other bill I was going to pay for from that older couple. Wow God!

One thing that did bother me a little was when we started talking about Jesus. She said, "Who are we to say that there is no other way to God besides Jesus?" What? Yes, this is a Christian pastor. The Bible is very clear on that subject.

How can you believe in Jesus, accept Him as your Lord and Savior, preach on that and then say that Jesus may not be the only way? That makes no sense to me at all!

God continues to bless me with places to sleep and eat and with people I meet along the way. Every time I need something God knows exactly what I need and gives it to me right when I need it. Not when I want it, but when I need it.

Chapter Twenty Eight
Uphill Battle

11:00 A.M.

I am reading Daniel 2 right now. I feel this story represents in present time what our government is doing. God appointed Barack Obama as our president, but without God included in our government the country will fall apart because there are so many different aspects of the law. Our government is trying to merge different kinds of "metal" to please everyone. That, as you can imagine, will never work. There is only one God, our Lord and Savior Jesus Christ.

It is like when Nebuchadnezzar built the statue out of different materials. It didn't stand and fell apart because the materials didn't mold together. This is what is happening to our country as we speak.

We cannot please everyone, practicing any religion. But when we please God he will heal the hearts of some and our government will be stronger because of it. When we please God He blesses us. If we want a strong country we need to rely on a strong God.

My legs are killing me today. It has been Uphill and downhill all day. My calves hurt very bad.

I was sitting at a Burger King today and met a guy who biked from Washington D.C. to Cumberland and back. There is a trail that goes all the way there. It would be cool to take but it's too far out of my way and I would be in the middle of nowhere a lot of the time.

1:00 P.M. Meadow Mountain

I am resting in a meadow on Meadow Mountain. Today is Sunday, a rest day. I am not going to push it too much today. I am laying here looking into the sky. It is pretty nice out right now. I feel so close to the sky, it is a really cool feeling, almost like I could touch the clouds. I can't really explain it but boy, is it cool.

I am really pondering about what God may want to do with Jenn and I. Is He leading us to work with youth? Should we be youth group leaders again? Or is there something else?

3:10 P.M.

Well, it's raining! This happens a lot in the mountains; it is really nice, then all of a sudden it starts to rain. I took shelter at a school but just felt weird about it. I am sitting at some fancy restaurant right now. I really don't fit in and everyone is looking at me. Oh, well, that and spending $3 on soup when you're not really hungry is better than walking in the rain.

As I continue reading Daniel, one thing that I am noticing is that God or gods were a big deal in Bible times, so big that when Nebuchadnezzar realized what God did he announced it! Could you imagine President Barack Obama announcing on TV during a State of the Union address that God saved our nation?

We as Americans forget this. We are so worried about our "rights" that we forget what separation of church and state was created for.

This does not mean that a government official cannot live a godly life or make Christ- like decisions. All this means is that our government cannot force anyone to practice a certain religion. We have taken out "rights" so far that our rights are being taken away from us. Wake up, America! We are living in a country with a Godless government!

The facts are the facts and if some people don't like it, then do something about it!

God didn't put us here to make friends; He put us here to share Christ. Not everyone will like it or accept it; the Bible never said they would. Sometimes Christ is not comfortable.

For those who think that following Christ is all peaches and cream, you're wrong! It's tough; people laugh at you, mock you and say bad things about you. God may just ask you to walk 650 miles during the fall in the rain. But I tell you what, it is so worth it! Jesus saved us through His death, and because we act like Him, we will be treated like Him. But our reward is in heaven, not here on Earth. Yes, we get blessed here on earth too, but that is not the point. The point is Jesus. How can we be like Jesus, and not get treated like He did? Do you really think He would let us off the hook that easy? Jesus goes through all the pain and death and we get all the rewards with none of the pain? The Bible says that followers of Christ will get persecuted. So why are we so surprised when it happens? We're sinners that's why. At the root we are all selfish sinners who want things to go our way. That's why we need Jesus!

6:00 P.M. Frostburg, Maryland

I was so tired and wet today walking through the mountains in the rain. I was praying for God to give me a ride. It was not really raining, more of a miserable drizzle. Anyway, I kept seeing this green work van pass me all day. Finally around 4:30-5:00 he stopped and asked where I was headed. I told him and he told me to get in. His ten- year-old son was in the front seat. There were no seats in the back, just a bunch of tools and pipes. So that's where I sat. No more than two minutes after I got in the van it started to downpour.

IF MY SHOES COULD TALK

One of those "can hardly see" downpours. He brought me to two motels but they were both full. So he drove me a couple miles up the road to this Days Inn. As soon as we pulled in the driveway it stopped raining. Wow, God's timing is perfect. I got what I prayed for right when God knew I needed it.

I just walked into the bathroom in the hotel room; they have a full-body bathtub. I so am taking a hot bath. That was probably more than you wanted to know.

11:00 P.M. Days Inn Maryland

I just got a phone call from Sharron; her husband didn't leave today like normal and wants to pick me up tomorrow morning. Praise God, I totally wasn't planning on that.

With this ride I will be in D.C. in time for the National Day of Prayer, Prayer Summit! God is awesome! I am so excited. Probably won't sleep tonight. I have to meet him under an overpass at 4:00 A.M., and I have to walk 1.5 miles to get there. I will need to leave my hotel room at 2:30 A.M.

10/1/12   12:36 A.M.

Still up. I'm trying to stay up all night so I make it to my pickup point. I don't want to sleep through my alarm. I did set two alarms though, just in case I fall asleep. Once I am dropped off I will be in Arlington, Virginia. I will walk to D.C. from there.

I walked down to McDonald's just so I would stay awake.

Page | 108

"Lord, I am thanking you for this ride to D.C.
I am now praying for a way into the Summit. Lord, I
also pray that I am able to pray for our president. I
pray all goes well with this ride from a guy I never
met before, I trust you and that all this is planned out
by You. I pray for wisdom in what to say, Lord.
Guide me, Lord, in all I do. I am starting a new
journey of 100% faith; I have no clue what to do in
D.C. I need you, Lord, to take me and use me.

10/1/12 2:30 A.M.

I did it. I stayed up all night! I think I have
enough time to leave at 3:00 A.M. I'm totally ready
to be in Washington, but at the same time I'm not
excited because I don't really know what to do once
I get there. I was praying for a ride to D.C. if God
wanted me there for the Summit and I got it. I'm just
a little anxious because I am meeting a guy at
4 A.M. in the dark under a bridge I have never met. I
met his wife but not him. This is the couple whose
house I slept at the other night who has the homeless
guy living with them and I was saved by the
tornado.

I am so tired right now! Well, I'm leaving, on
my way to the overpass. Next time I write I will be
in DC.

Chapter Twenty Nine
D.C.

9:10 A.M. Washington D.C.

I'm in D.C. It feels amazing to be here! I have already visited the Lincoln Monument, Vietnam and WWII memorials. I have gotten some amazing pictures because it was so early no one was around. This is such a busy and powerful place. People are jogging, walking, running and biking everywhere. The weather is perfect.

I contacted Gary; this is the guy I will be staying with while I am here. He is Lloyd's cousin. He will be picking me up soon.

I am excited and anxious to see what God has in store for me here.

The ride here was interesting. There were four guys in the truck. I, of course, knew none of them and I was cramped in the back with all of the luggage. I literally had like twelve inches to squeeze into.

There are a lot of school groups here today, like every day, I'm sure.

This feels like a whole new journey to me. I have no idea what to do now and no idea how to do it. I am totally leaving this in God's hands; I don't even know what to expect. At least when I was walking I could expect something.

I have not a clue how I am going to make a connection with the president, if that is even how God wants this to happen. I don't even know how to get to the Summit yet.

10:30 A.M. In front of the Washington Monument

I'm sitting here waiting for Gary, people watching. This guy almost took a lady down with his dog's leash. He was riding a bike and the dog was pulling him.

I am waiting to be picked up by a guy I don't know driving a white car; that doesn't help much.

It is really busy right now. The tourists have come out. It is the most perfect fall day. The sky is blue and the sun is out and has that fall smell in the air, you know, dry leaves and crisp air.

Oh, there is Gary, I think. Gotta go.

11:00 P.M. Gary and Donna's House, VA.

I spent the day with Gary today. We talked a lot about what I feel God has me doing. We talked a lot about teens and how I feel that God may be leading me in the direction of youth ministry.

Gary asked me if it would be okay for him to contact his church because they are looking for a youth pastor. I guessed it wouldn't hurt so I said sure. I went to the meeting and was basically offered a job! What, really. God, You don't really want us to move to D.C., do You? I would need a pretty huge confirmation from God through Jennifer if that is what He wants! That would be a big change in our life. I don't really think that is what God wants from us yet.

I ate dinner with Gary and Donna at a Mexican restaurant in town. They had pretty good food.

I am looking forward to tomorrow to see what God has planned.

10/2/12   8:20 A.M. Metro

I am on the Metro headed into Washington with Gary for some meeting. I am praying that God opens up some doors.

I am down to about $10, hoping Jenn gets money on my card today from checks I have received from people.

The Metro is very full; seating is cramped. People in D.C. are so in tune to what is going on in the government. I mean it makes sense but I guess I was amazed by the fact that it is all they really talk about.

As I'm sitting here looking around it is kind of funny how everyone is dressed in dresses and suits but wearing rain boots.

People here look so unhappy, so mundane and stuck in a rut. The train is full and I see no smiles. I am sitting next to a rather large and smelly woman.

9:15 A.M. Meetings

I sat in on meetings with Churches for Middle East Peace, Church World Service, EAD and National Religious Campaign against Torture.

There is a lot going on in D.C. with the church. One thing I did notice is that there is a lot of "Church" stuff going on but no Church. By that I mean there is no body; everyone is on their own agenda. It is like the church in D.C. has forgotten that we are all the church and all have the same goal and that is to serve Jesus.

5:30 P.M. Pho 14

All those meeting today and I really felt no connection with any of them. Trying to see what God had in mind with those.

I did a lot today. I toured the Capitol building, went to the Library of Congress, walked through the National Archive and saw the Constitution, Declaration of Independence and the Bill of Rights. I walked over to see the White House today, too.

I have a Metro card but have no idea how to use the Metro. There are so many different lines; I got confused so I just walked the 3 miles up town to Pho 14 which is the restaurant we are meeting at. Gary had some meetings that I couldn't attend so I toured D.C. and we are meeting back here.

I am still not sure what God wants me to do in D.C. He got me here in time for the Summit but without money to even get a ticket for it. I had to use the money Bob gave me for food and shelter from the rain.

"What do you want, God? How do you want me to pray for the president? He isn't even in town tomorrow. What do you want me to do? What am I here for? Please, God, I need clarity on this.

Please, God, I am pleading with you; hear my prayer for this nation. Please forgive everything we have done against you. Shine Your light on the faces of those who know You so that they can shine for You, God. Hear my prayer, oh Lord, for me, so that I may be effective for You here in D.C. Guide me, Lord, with wisdom and discernment in what You have me here for. I want to listen, Lord, but right now I feel broken. I feel defeated and I need your peace and mercy to fall on me, Lord.

7:15 P.M.

I ate Vietnamese food for the first time today. It was really good.

I am now at the World Premier of The Line, a film about world hunger put on by Sojourners World Vision and Bread for Life. These are some organizations Gary is connected with.

It is really cool to see all the different ministries going on here in Washington.

Chapter Thirty
Cookie Jar

10/3/12   11:00 A.M.

When I left I had no idea how I was going to get home. Lloyd had mentioned that he might be able to buy me a plane ticket home. I emailed him once in D.C. and he said that he wasn't able to because his money was tied up someplace else. I wasn't that worried; I knew God would get me home somehow. I got an email from Lloyd today asking how much I needed for a plane ticket because he found $200 in a cookie jar! My plane ticket cost $150. I'm flying home. Thank you, God! I am going home Sunday night.

Email: "Great is Thy faithfulness! Great is Thy faithfulness! Morning by morning new mercies I see; all I have needed Thy hand hath provided. Great is Thy faithfulness, Lord, unto me."
Tabitha

Chapter Thirty One
Open Door

10/3/12 11:00 A.M.

I am headed to Pentagon City this afternoon. I do not have enough money to buy a ticket to the Summit, but I trust God will open a door. He always does.

I wasn't planning on going today but felt led to go anyway, even with only $70, so I asked Gary to bring me to the train station. He was kind of shocked knowing I didn't have enough money.

11:00 P.M.

What a day! God opened up that door. I got into the Summit. I was in the 24-hour prayer room praying and felt led to go ask registration about a ticket. They said that all the dinners and tickets for tours were gone. I said I didn't really care about those I just wanted to get into the Summit. He said, "Well, that is only $50." Sweet, I had $70. God, you are awesome!

I met a lot of people today from all over the country. There are 300 of us here.

10/4/12   6:45 A.M.

I am on the train again headed back to Pentagon City. We are going to meet with Congress today.

I find it interesting that when I'm not "walking" I start to judge people again. I am no longer "in need of relationship." I feel bad about that. I pray that I stay open to all people. It is so easy wearing normal clothing to blend in. I don't want to blend in. Don't blend in!

Chapter Thirty Two
United States Government

4:30 P.M.

What a day. I got to pray inside of the Kennedy Caucus Room and prayed for our nation and our government inside the offices of Congressmen and Representatives from Montana. I have been able to share my story with a lot of people. God is moving here in D.C. I can feel it.

I was even asked to share my story from the stage at the conference tonight! So much is going on I can't write it all down.

One government staff member we prayed with, Ross, is a Christian and he even prayed for us. How cool was that?

One of the main trends I am picking up on for government staff members is that they want us to pray for unity in Washington. They say that there is a lot of fighting going on back and forth all the time, and people do things just because it is opposite of their opponent. That is not America, people. Come on, grow up, this isn't first grade; this is our country and our freedom we are talking about.

People from the Summit have been coming up to me and saying that they are calling home and having people pray for me. That is great. God is so good!

Chapter Thirty Three
Over the Top

10/5/12 9:00 A.M.

Gary let me use his senior Metro Pass this week. With that card the Metro is half price. Another blessing from God!

Oops. Gary and I went to get on the train this morning and we were going to share the card today but once on the train we realized that we wouldn't be getting off at the same location. So I had to go back and buy a pass for today. It kind of messed up Gary's card for a couple trips but we figured it out.

I feel Satan trying to enter my thoughts. "In the name of Jesus, leave me alone." He is trying to make me feel like "one of those," an over-exhausted follower of Christ but I'm not! There is no flattery or going over the top. I just follow Jesus; listen to the Spirit. I am having a hard time with some of the people here at the Summit who openly express in a loud and over-the-top manner in public. I feel they are trying to make a scene. There is a time and place for those actions. We need to learn how to have discernment in this area.

The two ladies I spent the day with yesterday drove me nuts. They were so panicked all day, worried that we wouldn't get where we needed to be on time. They were so scatterbrained and they seemed too showy to me.

"Lord, forgive me for any judgment I may pass on people. Let me be focused on You and not what others do. Forgive me, Lord, for forgetting what I'm here for and forgetting the lost and needy." It is amazing how easy it is to get caught up in "life." It's amazing to me how well we just blend in. We need to love the rich and the poor, the strong and the weak. We need to show the love of Jesus to all, regardless.

"Lord, help me to be more like Jesus to those around me. Give me wisdom and understanding in this so I can better serve You. Amen."

Wow! I just realized why God has been blessing me with money. I have been given a total of just over $300 since I have been in D.C.. I left Hamilton with just over $300! God wasn't blessing me with money for money; He was blessing me to show me that He has provided ALL my needs. Amazing. Thanks, God!

Yesterday as I was praying in the government offices I felt God say to me that my prayer for the president would be short and sweet, about thirty seconds long. I thought that was kind of weird. But today we had a prayer concert outside by the Washington Monument. The leader of that prayer concert came on stage and said this,

"We are going to do something a little different. We are going to open the stage up for prayer. Whoever feels led to come up and pray, please do so. You will have about thirty seconds." Hold on! Did I just hear that right? So I went up and prayed for the president. This was my prayer, "Matthew 19:26: For with man this is impossible, but with God all things are possible. Lord, allow President Barack Obama to see this. Amen"

I know that is how God wanted this to happen. Instead of my one prayer that I thought I was going to pray, more than 300 people prayed for our president that day!

After I got done praying, I felt an instant weight being lifted, the responsibility was over. It was the craziest feeling I had ever felt.

Chapter Thirty Four
Secret Agent Man

12:00 P.M.

Well, I am taking a break at Johnny Rockets in the mall. Now that I have done what I came here for I have a strange "completed" feeling. I am ready to go home.

I met a new friend today named Raymond. He is here for the Summit as well. We were walking around by the White House together talking and we noticed that there was fencing up close to the White House that wasn't there the day before. So we walked up to the guard there; we then realized he was a Secret Service Agent named Ron. We talked to him for a little and I asked if I could pray for him. He, with a surprised look on his face, said yes. So Raymond and I prayed for Ron. Then we walked around to the other side of the White House and met Ed, another secret service agent. Raymond asked if we could pray for him. (He really meant me.) Ed, again with a surprised look on his face said, "Uh, well, I can't close my eyes but yes." We thought that was pretty funny. So it was pretty cool that we got to pray for two secret service agents in front of the White House. Thanks, God, for that cool moment.

Chapter Thirty Five
Guest of Honor... Really?

10/6/12 8:30 A.M. On the Metro

On the Metro, again. I am headed to the Capitol. Yesterday I was called the guest of honor by a lady sitting at our table during the Summit dinner. I don't really feel like the guest of honor. I haven't really done anything more than they have. Yeah, I walked here, but people walk every day. Some of you reading this book probably walk more in thirty days at your job than I did to get here. Shoot, I am honored to be here with them. Out of how many people that could have been here there are only 300. I am among people of great faith. They chose to be here. They are all guests of honor.

9:30 A.M.

This journey is proof to me that when we act God acts.

I met Paul on the Metro this morning. He is from Australia. He asked me what I was doing so I got to share with him all that God has done. I even got to pray with him.

I got a ride to the Martin Luther King monument with a group from Kettering Baptist Church today.

Wow, what an amazing morning. First we all met over by the Capitol Building to have a prayer concert there; then we went over to the Martin Luther King Memorial for prayer and worship, OUTSIDE! There was a large group of people there. This was the first official prayer meeting at the monument. I felt like I was a part of history; it was awesome.

3:00 P.M.
I missed the Mt. Vernon Trip today. The busses were full. So I spent the afternoon by myself in DC riding around on the Metro and going to the mall again. I did get to meet some more people, though. I met Stephanie in the train station; her dad is a pastor. I also met Kathy in the mall at McDonald's, real nice lady. I am on my way back to the hotel now for our nightly conference. I am exhausted and ready to go home.

I have been invited to speak at a church in Las Vegas; that's cool, but I will leave that up to God. God is needed there, that's for sure.

Chapter Thirty Six
Going Home

10/7/12   5:40 A.M.

I'm going home! My biggest worry is that I forget, not what happened, but how to be like Jesus every day and to trust in him every day. Lord, help me to remember.

Romans 12:2 *"Don't copy the behavior and customs of this world, but let God transform you into a new person by changing the way you think. Then you will learn to know Gods will for you, which is good and pleasing and perfect."*

Some crazy things happened this week in D.C. One thing that was kind of funny to me was that there were a lot of people that asked if they could get their picture taken with me, people I had never met. I kind of felt like a famous person; it was strange. I am not really sure why they would want their picture taken with me, but okay.

I am excited to surprise my wife with what I am wearing. I got new dress shoes, dress pants, dress shirt and a bright orange tie. A lady at the Summit gave me money to buy new clothes so my wife could see me all dressed up. She is going to flip out. She thinks I will be wearing wind pants and a tee shirt. I love her so much and I think this journey has made that love even stronger. Jenn has been such a huge support. I could have never done it without her.

8:30 A.M.

Today Pastor John from Hamilton Christian Reformed Church is calling me at 10:00 am. At that time I will be in front of the White House leading his church in prayer for our nation. I pray this is a turning point for Hamilton.

I am really feeling led to pray the Lord's Prayer this morning. Not sure why, but it just feels right.

10:30 A.M.

God is . . . man, I don't even know what to say. Once Pastor John got me on the phone I shared with him that I felt led to pray the Lord's Prayer with them. You know what he said? That is what he was teaching on that week. Man that's crazy!

3:30 P.M.

I'm at the airport in Baltimore waiting for my flight. Gary and Donna drove me here. We went to church this morning and then went to get lunch. Gary and Donna have been such a blessing.

I am really bored right now. I have three hours until my plane leaves. I guess I will walk around the airport and people-watch a little. That is always fun. Come on, you know you do it, too.

Chapter Thirty Seven
I'm Home

10/8/12 My House

I am so excited to be home, but yet it is a little strange. I was confused this morning when I woke up, and a little scared when I realized that there was someone sleeping next to me (my wife). I forgot I was home.

It's kind of funny. I feel like my wife and I are dating again. I don't want to leave her or let her go!

It was so nice to eat breakfast with my family this morning. It felt so good to sit in my chair and watch my TV and see local news personalities. I know life will be different after this journey. I pray I do not forget what God has done and continues to do. I think the hardest part is making sure we keep that active faith going. Just because I am not "on a mission" right now doesn't mean God stops. I feel now is the time to share, to share with others of God's grace, mercy and love he has for us and gives us. I don't want to get into the normal routine of life. At the same time I have a family here at home. We are willing to do what God calls us to do but we need a lot of praying through. Please pray with and for us as we as a family try to figure out what God has for us next. There are a lot of things floating around out there and the last thing I want to do is get so busy I become ineffective. Praying is the answer; through prayer all things will be answered. God knows what we need and what is next, we just have to pray and listen to Him.

It feels weird being here at home with "nothing to do." I mean there are things to do but I was on such a mission for so long that I was focused. I now need to pray to refocus on what is next.

I am excited to go out with my wife this afternoon. We are going to have lunch at Crust 54, my best friend's new pizza joint in Holland, Michigan. He opened two weeks ago so I haven't even eaten there yet.

Then I have to go get a new Bible, as I gave mine away this last week. I can't go without that; I feel kind of lost and unarmed without it. I know whoever has it will love it, though.

I want to thank all of you for following what God is doing. Your comments and just the fact that I knew people where watching meant so much to me. It really kept me out there; it gave me purpose.

10/11/12

Well, it has been on my heart and mind for a long time. Since I have been home it has been brought up a half a dozen times. I think God is trying to tell me something.

I have applied to Liberty University for an associate degree in religion. We will see where it goes from there. I sent in my financial aid forms this morning.

Let's see what God does.

10/12/12   Lunch today

Had lunch today at Crust 54 with Pastor Doyle Passmore from Lakeshore House of Prayer. I will be sharing about my journey with his church on Oct. 28. There are also some other things in the works, too.

I stopped by Ridge Point today and was able to catch up with Aaron Brown a little bit today.

10/17/12

Lloyd and I had a great chance to talk today for a couple hours. Please pray for both of us and our families as we try to listen to God on how to move forward with what He has given us.

10/18/12   God's Faithfulness and Grace

We are called as followers of Christ not only to follow but to share with others about Christ and what He means to us and how He has changed our lives. He has changed my life!

Philippians 4:4-7 *"Always be full of joy in the Lord. I say it again-rejoice! Let everyone see that you are considerate in all you do. Remember, the Lord is coming soon. Don't worry about anything, instead pray about everything. Tell God what you need, and thank him for all he has done. Then you will experience God's peace, which exceeds anything we can understand. His peace will guard your hearts and minds as you live in Christ Jesus."*

I have started my book. Please pray that what is written honors God and displays the many ways He provides when we do what God has called us to do. I feel the book will display God's great faithfulness and grace. Even though we do not deserve anything, out of God's grace He gives.

10/19/12   Invitation to Pray

Every Wednesday there is a prayer meeting held at Hamilton Christian Reformed Church. For the next three weeks the prayer is going to be focused on praying for our nation and our government, two weeks prior to the election and the day after the election. We want to pray that God blesses our nation.

We want to pray that the election goes well and we want to pray after the election for our new president, whoever that may be.

The invitation is open to you. Please join us for the next three Wednesdays at 7 A.M.-8 A.M.

If you cannot join us at the prayer meeting I want to invite you to take a few moments at 7 A.M. to join in that prayer wherever you are.

Our nation needs prayer, not just one day a year on the National Day of Prayer, but constant prayer.

I know this is way early but I also want to invite you to the Hamilton area National Day of Prayer service. This will be held on the National Day of Prayer on May 2, 2013.

Ministry Opportunities

There is no way I could have made any of this happen. God is so good.

He opens doors we don't expect and closes doors we don't expect also.

The hard part is going through the right door. That's where prayer and discernment comes in.

I had another opportunity to share with the middle school students at The Gate ministry located inside Hamilton Christian Reformed Church. I think sometimes I go into something trying to reach the masses when sometimes all God wants is to touch one person. Sometimes we may never even know who we touched. I was very humbled yesterday when one of the students at The Gate last week came up to me. He shared with me that for one of their MEAP tests they had to write about someone that they would want to speak at their school. He said that he wrote about me. Crazy, never expected that. Out of all the people that are 'way more interesting than me and have done way cooler and better things than me? Why me?

I think that goes to show that we as followers of Jesus need to act like Jesus more often. We never know who is watching or listening. Who knows? Maybe someday that kid will be our president.

After sharing with the kids I was able to talk with Pastor John. He had a lot to share as well. He asked me to pray about being on the board of The Gate as they are planning on restructuring the program.

So please join me in prayer for that as well.

10/23/12   Liberty University

I should hear back today if I get accepted into Liberty University. I will be studying for my Associates in Religion. Please pray that everything goes through.

10/24/12   Accepted

It's official, I'm a college student! I have been accepted to Liberty University. I am enrolled for classes starting January 14. Praise Jesus! I am excited for this part of our journey.

10/26/12   Wednesday Prayer Meeting
Prayers For Our Government

We thank you, Father, for a government that is generally honest and trustworthy. We know our leaders have difficult decisions to make each and every day. Give them wisdom and ears to hear your voice. We pray, Lord, for our current president Barack Obama, that you will guide him in the work you have called him for, and that all our legislators will work together to do what is right for all. Amen.

Pray for our president and the work God has called him to do.

Pray for our legislators that they establish just laws that guide our nation.

Pray for our nation's judges that they will rule fairly and in accordance with God's will.

Pray for those who protect us (armed forces, police, firefighters, etc.).

Pray for protection from terrorist attacks.

Pray for our State of Michigan government leaders.

Pray for our schools and those who work in them, both public and private

I Timothy 2: 1-3 *"I urge you, first of all, to pray for all people. Ask God to help them; intercede on their behalf, and give thanks for them. Pray this way for kings and all who are in authority so that we can live peaceful and quite lives marked by godliness and dignity. This is good and pleases God our Savior."*

Romans 13:1-5 *"Everyone must submit to governing authorities. For all authority comes from God, and those in position of authority have been placed there by God. So anyone who rebels against authority is rebelling against what God has instituted, and they will be punished. For the authorities do not strike fear in people who are doing right, but in those who are doing wrong. Would you like to live without fear of the authorities? Do what is right, and they will honor you. The authorities are Gods servants, sent for your good. But they have the power to punish you. They are God's servants, sent for the very purpose of punishing those who do what is wrong. So you must submit to them, not only to avoid punishment, but also to keep a clear conscience."*

Lakeshore House of Prayer

I was blessed today with the opportunity to speak about obedience to God, and share what God did during my walk to D.C. and what He is continuing to do.

Pastor Doyle Passmore and the congregation at Lake Shore House of Prayer welcomed me with open arms. I was excited to hear from so many people how they were affected by my act of faith. I never expected so many people to be so impacted. That just goes to show that God can and will use anyone to do his work.

My family and I were so blessed in more ways than one by this experience today.

Thank you, Lake Shore House of Prayer, for inviting me and my family to share with you. May God continue to bless you and your ministry. The lunch after church was great too.

11/19/12   Youth Group
Last Journal Entry

I spoke at Trinity Reformed Senior High youth group last night. I think I was not letting God take over as much as I should have. I wasn't nervous but it was like I was back in high school wanting everyone to like me. I think I wanted to make an impression so badly I tried too hard. I didn't give it 100% to God.

Sometimes we think we are giving it to God but we really aren't. Life is much easier when we give it to God 100% and don't try to rely on ourselves for success but rely on God.

Epilogue

It has been almost a year since I took my walk to Washington D.C. My life has been forever changed. Today I still walk with God but in a completely different way than I have ever done before.

I am not walking with God because I think I have to but because I truly want to. I am walking with God because I love Jesus and I have a personal relationship with him. You see when we, followers of Christ, truly follow we walk with Jesus every day. Jesus becomes all we want. When we walk with Jesus we start to realize that life is not about us. Life is about Jesus Christ. Sharing who he is and what he has done for us. When we stop walking we lose track of Jesus. Jesus becomes a faded figure in the distance. Soon we lose track of Him all together. Yes, the walk can be long, uphill and downhill, but it's worth it. The walk is wonderful, exciting, energizing, life changing, and worth it.

When we put all our trust in God amazing things happen. Not only does God provide our needs but our faith and relationship with Him grows.

I learned through this journey that relying on God is truly easier than trying to do it on my own. I used to think all I needed to do was believe in Jesus and pray. I now know that I need a personal relationship with Him. Without a relationship I just know about Jesus. I need to know Jesus.

I will never stop walking with God. I can't stop walking with God. If I stop walking, I stop living. So I pray that if you haven't started walking with Jesus, start! Don't wait until tomorrow or when it is easy, start now. If you don't know Jesus find someone who does and ask about him. If you don't know anyone who knows Jesus call me. Jesus is the best thing that has ever happened to me and He can be that for you too.

So I want to say to you what I think Jesus would say to you. "Don't ever stop walking."

Prayer Requests

As this journey ends many more will begin. Please join us in prayer as we continue to listen to God and try to follow his direction.

Please continue to pray for Lloyd and myself as we are in prayer about another walk.

As ministry opportunities come our way please keep my family and I in your prayers as we need to discern what we should get involved with so we can be effective for the kingdom.

Pray for our nation, pray for the lost, pray for the broken, and pray for those on the frontline for Christ, pray for those doing His work in your town, church and schools.

Contact Info

Please contact me with any questions or if you would like to schedule a speaking engagement.

John- 616-510-1634
And yes this really is my phone number

Starting Point Sept. 3 2012

Outside Plainwell, MI, Good Old Americana

Lake Hudson, Hudson, MI

My sleeping quarters for the night on Lake Hudson, MI.

Having a good day.

Indian Trails Campground, Ohio

Downtown Wooster, Ohio

Mike and Kathy, Wooster, Ohio

24 hour prayer chapel, AKA mini church somewhere in PA.

It rained all day.

Peak of Mt. Washington PA

**Original bridge built by George Washington and his Army prior to his presidency.
Somewhere in PA**

En' route

Very tired but finally made it to D.C. Exactly 30 days into the walk!

Me in front of the White House.

Me with the "Jesus Lady"
She has been in D.C. for 30 years with a statue of Jesus outside the Capitol Building in Washington D.C.

National Day of Prayer Event

Praying in front of the Capitol Building

<u>Thoughts</u>

<u>Thoughts</u>

Thoughts